D1433600

THE CENTRAL SCHOOL OF SPEECH AND DRAMA
UNIVERSITY OF LONDON

CARIBBEAN
STYLE

CARIBBEAN STYLE

BY SUZANNE SLESIN & STAFFORD CLIFF,
JACK BERTHELOT, MARTINE GAUMÉ,
DANIEL ROZENSZTROCH
PHOTOGRAPHS BY GILLES DE CHABANEIX
FOREWORD BY JAN MORRIS

Thames and Hudson

TO NIUTA AND ROY TITUS,
ROSANNE AND BRENTON CLIFF,
CHRISTIANE, PASCAL, ANOUCK, AND SOPHIE BERTHELOT
PHILIPPE BARRIÈRE,
SONIA AND NATHAN ROZENSZTROCH,
AND CATHERINE, MARTIN, AND SIMON DE CHABANEIX

First published in Great Britain in 1985 by Thames and
Hudson Ltd, London. Originally published in the United
States in 1985 by Clarkson N. Potter, Inc., 201 East 50th
Street, New York, New York 10022.

Reprinted in 1986, 1987, 1988, 1989, 1990, 1992, 1995, 1996

British Library Cataloguing-in-Publication Data

A catalogue record for this book is available from the
British Library

ISBN 0-500-23455-8

Printed and bound in Japan

ACKNOWLEDGMENTS

Jack Berthelot and his interest in the architectural heritage of the Caribbean was the starting point for *Caribbean Style*. An architect based in Point-à-Pitre, Guadeloupe, Berthelot and his associate Martine Gaumé had in 1982 produced *Kaz Antiyé: Jan Moun Ka Rété (The Caribbean Popular Dwelling)*, Editions Perspectives Créoles.

When, later that year, the book became the catalog for an exhibit at the Centre National Georges Pompidou in Paris, Berthelot invited Daniel Rozensztroch, a French journalist, and Gilles de Chabaneix, a photographer, to tour and record the Lesser Antilles. The islands they visited in the summer of 1983 included Guadeloupe, Marie Galante, and Les Saintes, Martinique, Barbados, Antigua, Nevis, and Montserrat. In September, the group joined forces with Suzanne Slesin in New York and Stafford Cliff in London to produce this book, and it was then decided to add some of the islands of the Greater Antilles. A second trip to Jamaica, Haiti, and Puerto Rico was organized in the spring of 1984, when the Lesser Antilles island of St. Barthélémy was also included.

Unfortunately, Berthelot died tragically in an accident in Guadeloupe in July 1984, and although his knowledge and point of view played an essential role in the book's development, he never saw its completion. We hope that *Caribbean Style* is to his standards.

We are particularly grateful to all the people who made it possible for us to photograph their homes, often without much prior warning. Our thanks go also to:

Luce Eeckman, who made the first connections;

Jill Sheppard, Franklin Margretson, and the other members of the Caribbean Conservation Association who provided help on all the islands;

the members of The Association Guadeloupienne pour la Sauvegarde de l'Architecture dans la Caraïbe, who supported and encouraged this project;

Jan Morris, who wrote the foreword; Michael Steinberg, who translated the introduction; and Max Le Superbe, who did the architectural drawings; and Ian Hammond who did all the tracings.

In addition, we wish to thank: Howard Angione, Antoine Bootz, Terri Cafaro, Campaign Colour Laboratories, Nigel Clayton, Eryc Eclinval, Leyland Gomez, Jean-Paul Hervieu, Obelin Jolicoeur, Laboratoire Dupon, Yannick and Philippe Lahens, Danièlle Letellier, Richard Lupinacci, Frances Murray, Desmond Nicholson, Panda Photographic, Andrew Pettit, Jane Rosen, Paula Semelmacher, Inda Schaenen, John Scott, Kathe Telingator, Ed Vivero, Helen Walker, and Françoise Winter;

Our agent Lucy Kroll, and our publisher and the staff at Clarkson N. Potter, who include Alan Mirken, Bruce Harris, Carol Southern, Michael Fragnito, Gael Dillon, Lynne Arany, Teresa Nicholas, Robin Feldman, Harvey-Jane Kowal, and especially our editor Nancy Novogrod.

Suzanne Slesin, New York; Stafford Cliff, London; Martine Gaumé, Pointe-à-Pitre; Daniel Rozensztroch, Paris; Gilles de Chabaneix, Paris

February 1985

CONTENTS

FOREWORD

JAN MORRIS

At first thought the very phrase "Caribbean style" seems a contradiction in terms. How can a single style emerge out of a scattered heterogeneous archipelago, spread over hundreds of miles of sea, without a common language, culture, history or even geology?

Some of the Caribbean islands are spiky and volcanic, some are coral, low-lying in the ocean. Some are open to the wild Atlantic, some bask sheltered in the lee. They have been variously ruled by the French, the Spaniards, the English, the Dutch, the Danes and the Americans, and some indeed have been passed so repeatedly from sovereignty to sovereignty that they are a positive mish-mash of influences and memories; while the great black majority of the populace, descended from African slaves, have acquired over the generations a myriad ethnic strains and symptoms, from the high cheekbones of the original Carib Indians to the commanding postures of European aristocrats.

A Caribbean style! It seems at first thought about as definable as the human condition itself.

Yet when I consider the matter deeper, I perceive several *sub*-styles, so to speak, which can be ascribed to the Caribbean region as a whole: and the first is the Style of Climate.

Most of us, I suppose, when we think of those tropic seas, think first of climate: sunshine to warm the waters and illuminate the beaches, trade winds to rustle the statutory palms, humid warmth to encourage the coconuts, the sugarcane, and the paw-paw. But actually the Caribbean climate is more than just a divine convenience, or even a builder of character. It is, more than any other climate I know, an aesthetic in its own right, an abstraction of immense sensual power, as full of emotional suggestion and allusion as a work of art.

Its magnificent storms, whipping the tall palms and drenching the rough grass lawns, are exactly like the sudden volatile passions of a hot human temper, and the warm calm that invariably follows them, making the wet foliage steam, almost *purr* with luxurious relief, is like a figure of forgiveness and reconciliation. As for the high blue skies, sometimes smudged so aerily with cumuli, sometimes banked brooding with storm-clouds, they are extraordinarily and sometimes all too disturbingly suggestive of eternity.

And this meteorological art-form, as it were, has inescapably governed the manner of Caribbean living — not just physically in verandahs and wide eaves, or houses left open to breeze and sunshine, but in ways more subtle: in a kind of genial *non far niente*, almost fatalistic, which obtains in most Caribbean arrangements, grand or simple, and which makes one feel always among the buildings and artifacts of these islands that life is essentially transience, that storms will pass, furies fade, leaving always, whatever happens, that towering implacable sky above.

There is a Style of the Caribbean Substance, too. By and large things in these islands, when they are not made of steel or concrete, are made of lovely materials — warm, tropic, easy-going, mellow matters. There is pink coral out of the sea, and plank bleached by wind and sun, and glorious teak from the forests of the mainland, and old silver from the cultures of vanished Empires, and palm-frond, and bird-feather, and gay cotton out of the African past, and rope of harbor-front, and rattan of woodland, and pumice of hot volcano.

Though you may find all these substances elsewhere, though they have been assembled in these seas, not organically, but as the flotsam of history, still it is only here that you may experience them in quite such piquant conjunction. It is a mélange not always harmonious, not always beautiful as a matter of fact, but it does constitute, for better or for worse, a discernible stylistic alliance.

Then of course there is the Style of Purpose. There is no pretending that the functions of the Caribbean have generally been very inspiring.

Except for the Caribs, whose now insubstantial presence still drifts figuratively through the archipelago, the people of the islands went there in the first place either in search of power and wealth, or because they were obliged to. No Pilgrim Fathers reached these landfalls, no idealistic refugees from tyrannies of State or Church. Slaves, slave-masters, moneymakers and hedonists — such have been the shapers of Caribbean society, as of Caribbean forms.

This makes for something at once showy and down-to-earth in the feel of the region. On the one hand we have the grand display of the planters, the burghers and the idle expatriates, generally suggesting, however splendid of artifact or lovely of texture, some tinge of nouveau-riche; on the other, the blunt, simple, often makeshift idioms of the poor people.

Yet the two elements are interchangeable, too: for the rich of the Caribbean, however rich, have been obliged by climate and circumstance to create solidly rather than delicately, in shapes more bold than tender: while conversely the works of the poor have been elevated always by the gaiety, the fantasy and the exuberance of the African tradition.

And actually, the more I think about it, the more I recognize a kind of unity in the very variety of the Caribbean. This is the very opposite of a continental landmass, the antithesis even of a consolidated state or nation. There is nothing remotely monolithic to it; it is all shift, stipple, contrast, dapple and disparity.

Does it really add up to one, definable Caribbean Style? Perhaps not in the exact fact, or the particular object: but as I summon into my mind all the dazzling images of those seas, all the hints and secret scents of the spice-and-sugar places, I perceive it most distinctly as a style in the imagination — and out of many imaginations, living and dead, it has reached now a more formal unity in the pages of this book.

JACK BERTHELOT
AND MARTINE GAUMÉ

INTRODUCTION

The Caribbean. The place immediately brings to mind specific colors, arranged in a specific way. Blue above, blue below. White for the beach, green for the coconut palms. Dominating all, the gold of the sun. This book will add to that palette the colors and shades of the lives of a people seen through their homes.

All West Indians, whether they live on the Bahamas to the north or the Greater or Lesser Antilles to the south, are the descendants of transplanted peoples. Between 1492 and 1504, Christopher Columbus made four voyages to the Antilles, the string of islands that separate the Atlantic Ocean from the Caribbean Sea. Arcing from midway between southern Florida and the Yucatán Peninsula to just off the coast of Venezuela, the Antilles include the larger northern islands of the Greater Antilles — Cuba, Jamaica, Haiti/Dominican Republic, and Puerto Rico — and the smaller southern islands of the Lesser Antilles — among them, Antigua, Guadeloupe, Nevis, Montserrat, Martinique, Barbados, Grenada, and Trinidad. Although Columbus was trying to reach India, he discovered in the islands the gateway to the New World. Throughout the next century, Spaniards lured by dreams of gold were the primary conquerors of the Caribbean. Then, slowly, the English and French began to colonize the Lesser Antilles, which the Spaniards had ignored. From the 1600s until the mid-19th century, millions of enslaved Africans were convoyed to the islands. Oth-

ers emigrated from far-off Asia. All were forced to reeducate themselves in order to survive. The conditions they met were often unbearable, but out of their struggles and efforts a Creole culture and a Creole way of life were born.

The first colonists who debarked in the Caribbean found themselves in a totally unknown universe. They had no idea which crops to cultivate (perhaps they waited months for winter to come before realizing that the climate was continually hot and humid). Native Indians tried to help the foreigners, even though the newcomers were anxious to exterminate them. In the Lesser Antilles, the colonists encountered Indians of the Carib tribe, who had driven their predecessors, the Arawaks, from the islands. In the Greater Antilles, the Indians they met were known as Tainos, descendants of the Arawaks. Nothing remains of these Indians except a few tools and some of their savoir faire. Their shelters, called *carbets* and *ajoupas,* were well suited to the climate, becoming antecedents for contemporary Creole houses which are topped by broad protective roofs. Fresh air circulates freely underneath them, cooling the interiors.

The early settlers built only temporary shelters. They clung to the idea of one day returning to their homelands. But with the development of the sugar trade, permanent homes were constructed. The grandest houses in the Antilles were built with wealth derived from sugarcane. Many of them have completely disappeared or fallen into ruins. Those that remain are fragile relics of a bygone world and are today in danger of disappearing with the death of the sugar trade.

To become familiar with the people of the Caribbean, it is not sufficient merely to enter the homes of the upper classes. The houses of townspeople and peasants, as well as buildings created in the service of colonial powers — forts, barracks, and churches — have stories to tell.

The architecture of the Antilles is the outgrowth of baroque mixtures of the styles brought to the islands by different peoples. The short span of time that has passed since the arrival of the first colonists helps to explain some of the charm of West Indian decor, which comes from a certain naïveté. When looking at West Indian houses — from grand plantation houses to modest wooden *cases* — one is immediately struck by their fresh, lively character. They join together the spatial lightness of wood and the refinement of ornament and color. This architecture, which seems merely spontaneous, is still quite young. Naturally, it displays the qualities of youth.

Perhaps in memory of the slave whose cabin was a refuge for privacy, West Indians declare their love for their homes with the delicate frills and lacework that adorn galleries and interiors. The façade of a typical Barbadian "dollhouse" is invaded by apertures in a pattern as rigorous as those of monumental architecture. Everywhere, Christmas wreaths that last all year, children's balloons, and highly colored prints enliven the interiors of simple residences just as the exteriors of houses on the English-speaking islands are brightened by sharp, lively colors. All of this exuberance is even more noticeable because it is set off against a strict graphic background: the horizon and vertical lines of the gallery, the parallel lines of corrugated metal and of window shutters.

The first characteristics of a truly Caribbean style appeared during the 18th century. But it was only in the following century that a fully coherent, specifically Caribbean architecture developed. Today's West Indian houses are amalgams of scholarly architecture on the one hand and, on the other, the architecture of the countrysides of both Europe and Africa. Thus, within one luxurious house can be found windows ordered in a totally Palladian manner and doors closed with wooden latches based on African designs.

The architectural style developed by borrowing from the different cultures that were in contact throughout the Caribbean. The elements of Creole architecture that can be traced to the colonists include jalousie shutters and the symmetrical composition of façades organized around a central entrance. Some characteristics can be more specifically identified with one or another colonizer. The French brought dormer windows which allow air to circulate under the roof. Only in the islands colonized by the English is the taste for porches widely prevalent — a small projecting form that decorates and protects the entranceways. The Spanish, in adapting to the needs of the climate, built houses of very simple forms using only doors and windows for ventilation. In consequence, the Spanish houses acquired unusual height.

Other characteristics found in Creole architecture were developed to satisfy the production needs of the large plantations. On many of the islands, the worker's cabin, which was part of the estate, had to be transportable. This enabled the workers to live in proximity to the field in which they were actually working. The custom of transporting cabins has been preserved, and modular cabins with standardized dimensions that facilitate relocation continue to be built.

Finally, some characteristics were provided by the black populations who were brought over in slavery. As in Africa, the blacks of the Antilles preferred darkness in the interiors of their cabins and closed them hermetically. This fact was commented upon by early chroniclers of the islands. According to Jean Baptiste du Tertre, the cabins were "shut like a box." This African custom was reinforced by the circumstances of slavery. The slave had nothing that really belonged to him. The interior of his house was the single element of his life over which he had some control.

The architecture of the Caribbean is a synthesis of different influences. Each island brings to it a unique personality. To the attentive viewer, each island has intrinsic characteristics that distinguish it from the others. As proof of this, it suffices to note the numerous differences between the houses of Guadeloupe and those of Martinique, particularly in the foundations and the rhythms of the façades. And yet these islands have parallel histories. They were colonized by the same nation and the same ethnic groups settled on them. On each island, the same mixture produced different effects and assumed different qualities.

The architectural style developed at the same time as a life style that was specifically Caribbean. The architecture of the Caribbean is first and foremost an architecture for life out-of-doors. Daily activities take place in spaces that are mostly outside the framework of the house itself. And even the framework is open to the outdoors, offering protection only from the sun and rain. Furthermore, that which is called the house often consists of several buildings. For example, the kitchen and the water cabin (which was used for doing the dishes and bathing) were freestanding buildings, independent of the main dwelling.

In hot climates, there are many hours when it is more pleasant to be outside than inside. Buildings became a background canvas for a composition in which the garden is as precisely laid out as the house itself. Between these two domestic areas — *extra muros* and *intra muros* — the gallery is an organic link, interior and exterior at the same time. It is not surprising that it is the decorative showplace of the house.

The house and its surroundings, the architecture, the furniture, and the garden reflect the Caribbean sensibility and the order of society. Thus, the expressly desired discomfort of the sofa on which one sits while waiting to be received by the master of the house; the whispers and mumbling voices that can be heard through thin, wooden partitions; the sensuality of exotic veined woods, richly scented and warm in tone. All are part of the seductiveness of a decor that hides and reveals at the same time — the shutters that shield an inquisitive stare; the row of doors that let in light and that sometimes frame a momentary scene uncovered in passing.

Caribbean style represents a vernacular architecture without official agreement or approval. It is not involved with learned concepts and does not frequent the seats of academe. It is a truly living style and is the fruit of experience. The diverse components group themselves as for a painting. Above the thickets, the royal palms, which once provided wood for construction, are evidence of long-gone settlements. The tamarind, which offers restful shade, and whose fruit is rich in vitamin C, is planted today, as long ago, between the house and the kitchen. Ever-useful medicine plants shelter themselves behind the wall of the same kitchen.

This book is certain to be a surprise for West Indians themselves. They live on their own islands, in exile from all the other islands. Each island is considered by its inhabitants a world unto itself, the far-off colony of a Western power. They are not acquainted with one another and, in any case, they believe that what is best in themselves comes from Europe or elsewhere. In these pages, West Indians will discover an undeniable, deep-rooted common Creole heritage.

It is their Creole identity that unites these cultures born in the conquest of the New World and anchored in islands of the Americas. Their wealth is drawn from their diversity.

RIGHT: Le Diamant, an enormous rock off the coast of Martinique, is one of the island's landmarks.

1

THE LOOK OF THE CARIBBEAN

The Caribbean offers a series of memorable, colorful, and ever-changing scenes in which the striking images of the idealized landscape are juxtaposed with the vibrancy of everyday life.

ABOVE: *Fresh fruits and vegetables on sale by the roadside include pineapples, eggplants, cucumbers, soursops, and mangoes.*

LEFT: *Fishermen in Martinique, oxen pulling a cart on Marie-Galente, and the crowded Haitian marketplace are among the typical Antillean scenes.*

LEFT AND RIGHT: *Nestled among palm trees, situated by the water, or set atop a hill, the Caribbean house is an intrinsic part of the varied landscape.*

ABOVE: *A verandah on Nevis overlooks a lush garden and offers a cool place to sit.*

ABOVE: *On Barbados, a terrace provides an uninterrupted view of the ocean as well as a space that is protected from the sun.*

14

Caribbean vegetation changes relatively little during the course of the year. The trees are always green and only a few flowers and fruits have distinct seasons. The coconut palm, a ubiquitous symbol of the Antilles, was originally imported from India.

LEFT: From the traveler's-tree, far left, which collects water at the base of its leaves, to the striking tree ferns, lychee trees, below far left, and huge water lilies, the plants and flowers on the different islands are as colorful as they are bountiful.

RIGHT: A group of palm trees on Nevis is reflected in a freshwater pond.

LEFT: *Fields of eggplant grow right up to a cluster of popular houses on the island of Haiti.*

RIGHT: *The method of agriculture follows the terrain of the islands. Stone fences delineate the fields on St. Barthélémy.*

BELOW RIGHT: *Vegetables are grown on the terraced mountains of Haiti.*

BOTTOM RIGHT: *Sugarcane is cut by hand on the gentle slopes near the sea on Martinique.*

2
OUTSIDE VIEWS

In the towns and throughout the countryside, the Caribbean offers a changing and varied architectural landscape. Brightly painted fences, decorative balconies, half-open shutters, and ornately gabled roofs are elements that both contrast with and complement the luxuriant vegetation.

ABOVE: The extravagantly peaked roof of a house in Haiti is an example of the fancifulness that is characteristic of many of the structures on the island.

LEFT: Delicate wood fretwork embellishes the façade of a two-tone house on Barbados.

BALCONIES AND VERANDAHS

The town balcony is the equivalent of the country verandah or gallery — an open-air spot where one can enjoy the breeze. On islands of French and Spanish influence, balconies always directly overlook the street, and people frequently use them to converse with their neighbors. By contrast, balconies and verandahs on the English-speaking islands tend to be more intimate. They are often enclosed and sometimes hidden at the side or rear of the house.

ABOVE: In Pointe-à-Pitre, Guadeloupe, wrought-iron balconies decorate the shuttered windows of a city house.

ABOVE LEFT AND LEFT: A gate, a garden, a stair leading up to the entrance, and an enclosed verandah are typical of houses on Barbados.

ABOVE: *Geometric wooden railings line the balconies of a house in Grand Bourg, on the island of Marie-Galante.*

RIGHT: *The imaginatively carved wooden balustrade and the checkerboard pattern on the roof and sides of the dormer window enliven a simple house in St. Claude, on Guadeloupe.*

RIGHT: *The use of brick and the wrought-iron balconies of a house in Point-à-Pitre are rare in Guadeloupe.*

LEFT: *The open second-floor balcony of a town house in Grand Bourg on Guadeloupe is typical of that island.*

RIGHT: *Open or enclosed, made of prefabricated metal or carved wood, a variety of balconies and verandahs decorate the city and country houses of Montserrat, Guadeloupe, Antigua, and Haiti.*

DECORATIVE TRIM

Because it filters the bright sunlight and still allows air to pass through, the cutout trim on the majority of Antillean houses is as functional as it is decorative. No two houses are the same. Each is the personal expression of its prideful owner.

LEFT: *At Gustavia, on the island of St. Barthélémy, a fishing theme is reflected in the border of fish and seagulls.*

RIGHT: *Stylized columns, cutout stars on a balcony, a Greek-key frieze, and lacelike clerestory window panels are some of the motifs used as trim.*

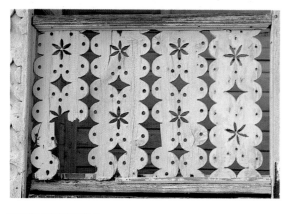

PITCHED ROOFS

The peaked roof is the most important element of architecture in the Caribbean. Like a large umbrella, it protects the occupants of the house from the sun as well as the rain, and represents a sense of security. The thatch and wood-shingled roofs of the past are being replaced by corrugated iron, the most widely used roofing material on the islands today.

FAR LEFT AND BELOW FAR LEFT: Identical peaked roofs are typical architectural details on the English-speaking islands. The two peaks are on a small shingled house on Nevis, the trio on a house in Montserrat. Each roof represents the addition of a room to the original house.

LEFT AND BELOW LEFT: The two wood houses that date from the 1920s in Didier, a residential quarter in Fort-de-France, Martinique, feature peaked roofs.

RIGHT: The extravagantly peaked roof in Port-au-Prince, Haiti, crowns the turn-of-the-century town house.

27

ISLAND COLORS

Before paint was made widely available in the Antilles, the colors of the houses were determined by the raw materials — dry straw and natural wood — that were used to build them. Paint became a common imported item in hardware stores between the two world wars, and bright colors soon replaced the natural hues. The new colors reflected the Caribbean surroundings: the intense blue of the sky, the red and yellow of the croton leaves, the pink of the bougainvillea.

Whether the candy colors of the houses on the English-speaking islands, the softer tones used on many of the islands of French influence, or the vibrant hues that are typical of Haiti, color is an essential part of the domestic landscape.

LEFT: *Hot pink, bright yellow, vibrant turquoise, and luminescent lilac are some of the colors of island buildings.*

RIGHT: *The yellow and red shutters contrast with the bright blue walls of this popular house on Montserrat.*

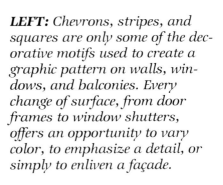

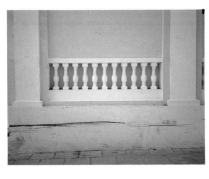

32

RIGHT: A two-story house in the town of Port-au-Prince, on Haiti, is a play of turquoise and white.

3

ISLAND INFLUENCES

In the Antilles, houses are sited and domestic activities planned so as to take advantage of the dominant trade winds—winds that blow constantly from the east to the west, bringing with them a freshness that is indispensable to life on the islands.

ABOVE: *The round shuttered window below the peak of a pink painted house on Haiti lets air into the attic.*

LEFT: *A grove of tall coconut palms sways in the wind near the port of Jacmel in Haiti.*

LIVING OUTSIDE

The gallery or verandah is the Caribbean islands' response to the climate as far as houses are concerned. Neither an indoor nor outdoor space, the gallery provides a separation between the brightness and heat of the outside world and the coolness and modulated light of the interior.

Louvered wood shutters on windows and doors, which are used instead of glass throughout the islands, control the light yet allow the interior of the houses to capture the cool breezes.

LEFT: *Louvered windows, shutter-lined verandahs, and open balconies are some of the architectural responses to the balmy Caribbean climate.*

RIGHT: *At the Weatherhills estate on Antigua, an open system of clerestory gratings allows air to circulate through the second-floor bedroom corridor of the main house.*

MATERIAL CONSIDERATIONS

Wood is the most important building material in the Antilles. In the past it was used almost exclusively, but wood is now more often seen in combination with other materials, such as brick, corrugated steel, and cement. The traditional town house more than any other structure offers a practical lesson in materials. The ground floors are of stone, the upper floors of wood. The stone is more impervious to fire, the wood more resistant to potential earthquakes.

LEFT: Braided twigs, flat steel, wood shingles, corrugated iron, bricks, bamboo, reinforced cement, and natural or painted wood are all common building materials.

RIGHT: The painted wood shutters are surrounded by pale yellow picture-frame windows at Trois Ilets on Martinique.

SUGARCANE

The richest and best lands of the Caribbean were given over to the cultivation of sugarcane — and the sugarcane plantations that began in the mid-17th century became the principal source of wealth for the islands.

After 1850, the plantations began to change in nature. The new methods of processing the sugarcane decentralized the traditional estates. While the sugarcane was still cultivated on the property, it was taken to factories to be refined industrially.

Only a few of the oldest plantations in the Antilles are still engaged in growing sugarcane. And although no longer in operation, the original buildings of the sugar refinery — today often in ruins — remain a rich source of architectural and cultural history.

TOP AND ABOVE: *The main house of La Ramée, on Guadeloupe, dates from 1930 and is part of a plantation that grows sugarcane processed in one of the four remaining factories on the island.*

TOP: *The estate of Fonds Saint Jacques, on Martinique, once an important sugar plantation, was remodeled at the turn of the 18th century by Père Jean Baptiste Labat, the famous chronicler who lived and traveled in the Antilles at that time.*

LEFT: *Sugarcane is cultivated on the flatlands of the estate.*

ABOVE: *The stone wall and the system of canals are all that remains of the original factory.*

WINDMILLS

The windmill was the pride of the sugarcane estate. Like mills powered by water or animals, it became obsolete in the mid-19th century with the development of advanced industrial methods for refining sugarcane. Now, abandoned, overgrown with vegetation or restored, the windmill is an evocative symbol of the past importance of the sugarcane plantation.

ABOVE: *Because it was situated on a small hill, the mill at Petit Canal, Guadeloupe, could profit from the wind.*

ABOVE LEFT: *The abandoned windmill is in Les Grands Fonds de Ste. Anne on Guadeloupe.*

LEFT: *The stone windmill is one of the most important features of the archeological site of the Galways plantation on Montserrat.*

ABOVE: *An unusual restored windmill on Guadeloupe has blades that mistakenly turn against the wind.*

RIGHT: *The windmill on an estate on Grande-Terre, Guadeloupe, is no longer in operation, but a cart pulled by oxen still carries the sugarcane to the nearby factory.*

COFFEE GROWING

After sugar, the second most important crop in the Antilles was coffee. Coffee plantations were at their most productive during the second part of the 19th century. And because the cultivation of the coffee bean requires a cooler climate than that of the sugarcane, it was usually grown on the more sheltered leeward slopes of the mountains.

TOP: The main house of La Pagésie, at Pointe Noire, on Guadeloupe, is part of a plantation that has cultivated both sugarcane and coffee.

ABOVE: The two-story house has a wood frame structure.

RIGHT: Set on a hill, the building is surrounded by groves of coffee trees.

RIGHT: *At La Grivelière, a coffee plantation on Guadeloupe that dates from the late 19th century, the small houses for the workers are grouped near the main plantation house.*

BELOW RIGHT: *After the coffee beans are picked, they are opened and laid out to dry on the glacis, a wide terrace in front of the house.*

LEFT: *In a second operation, the coffee beans are roasted in specially built ovens.*

DEVELOPING THE LAND

At one time, forests covered all the islands in the Caribbean. Volcanic eruptions, as well as erosion by the ocean, wind, and rivers, changed the tropical landscape. Over the centuries, agriculture developed on two contrasting scales — the vast plantations developed by the colonialists on the flatlands and the small plots nurtured by the inhabitants on the hilly terrains.

ABOVE: *A Haitian farmer surveys the expansive view from the small garden near his house.*

ABOVE LEFT: *Houses, each in the middle of its own field, dot the arid countryside in Haiti.*

LEFT: *A man turns over the earth on a deeply furrowed Haitian field.*

ABOVE: *On Haiti, a man is half hidden in a grove of mango trees.*

RIGHT AND BELOW RIGHT: *Small houses are surrounded by fruit trees, breadfruit trees, and coconut palms that provide not only food but shade as well.*

BRICKMAKING

La Poterie, a brick factory at Trois Ilets on Martinique, is one of the few estates in the Caribbean that is nonagricultural.

Bricks and tiles were originally brought to the islands as ballast on the Dutch ships that returned to Europe laden with sugar. Later, brick factories — of which La Poterie is among the few remaining examples — were established on the islands whose soil had the right clay content for the manufacture of the material.

TOP: The brick factory is a series of low buildings with corrugated metal roofs.

ABOVE LEFT: The plantation house of La Poterie is set on a hill overlooking the entrance to the harbor at Fort-de-France.

ABOVE: Louvered wood windows line the side of the addition to the main house built in the 19th century.

ABOVE: Rudimentary showers, with blue-and-white tiled floors, were part of an earlier modernization effort.

TOP: The roof tiles and wall bricks were made on site.

ABOVE: A metal structure is the main support of the wood house.

4

FOREIGN INFLUENCES

The search for gold brought Europeans to the Caribbean in the 16th century. Abandoning hope of finding gold in the Antilles, some stayed on as colonists and learned to adapt to their new surroundings.

The Creole culture, with its amalgam of architectural styles that developed over the next three centuries, reflects the synthesis of different peoples — from the plantation owners of European descent to the slaves they brought from Africa.

ABOVE: *The fanciful fretwork and curved balconies of a private house on Haiti are a new interpretation of the original turn-of-the-century Victorian detailing.*

LEFT: *The façade of Murat, a stone plantation house on Marie-Galante, is a provincial interpretation of French classicism.*

EARLY INFLUENCES

The most modest Antillean houses still resemble those the early settlers made from natural materials, using the techniques of the Africans and Amerindians, the earliest inhabitants of the Caribbean islands. These small handcrafted houses, with walls of braided twigs known as wattles, were once numerous on all the islands, but are slowly disappearing.

TOP AND ABOVE: *The roofs and sides of some houses on Haiti are made of royal palms, a building material that was already being used by the Amerindians. The palm fronds are made into thatch roofs, the trunks into walls.*

OPPOSITE ABOVE AND BELOW: *The braiding technique used for the walls of the two houses on Marie-Galante was originally brought to the islands by slaves from West Africa.*

SPANISH IDEALS

The earliest colonialists in the Caribbean, the Spaniards, settled for the most part in the Greater Antilles. Elaborate wrought-iron detailing, ceramic-tiled floors and walls, and balconies that extend from smooth plaster façades are some of the Caribbean architectural elements that reflect Spanish characteristics.

OPPOSITE AND TOP: *The white-and pastel-walled 18th-century houses in San Juan, Puerto Rico, feature wood and wrought-iron cantilevered balconies that give the buildings their Spanish look.*

ABOVE LEFT: *The high-beamed ceilings and arches in the corridor of a house in San Juan are typical features of Spanish houses.*

ABOVE RIGHT: *Glazed ceramic tiles decorate the stair risers in a San Juan residence.*

CRAFTED WITH IMAGINATION

The popularity of the gingerbread fretwork that was widely adopted on turn-of-the-century town houses in the Antilles was due to the invention of machines in the United States that could sculpt the wood in multiples. It was on the islands of Haiti and Trinidad that the decorative possibilities — inspired by Victorian examples — were given a verve and imaginative expression of their own.

ABOVE: *A colonnaded verandah surrounds a small house on Haiti. The bell-shaped tower is a typically Haitian detail.*

OPPOSITE ABOVE: *Cutout fretwork lines the eaves of a peaked-roof house on Haiti.*

OPPOSITE BELOW: *The white lacelike delicacy of the balcony railing as well as the panels over the door and window contrast with the bright blue trim of the Port-au-Prince residence.*

ENGLISH MANNERS

In the 18th century, when French residences were still usually of modest proportions, many a "great house" on the English islands was known for its elegance and comfort. These grand houses, of which Governor's House on Montserrat is a good example, were not built all at one time but, rather, were often the result of a series of separate structures.

TOP: *The Governor's House on Montserrat was built in 1750 and restored in 1907 after being damaged by a cyclone.*

ABOVE: *A ceiling fan was installed in the living room, which has been furnished with chintz-covered seating.*

OPPOSITE: *Arched doorways frame the view into the formal dining room of the house.*

FRENCH STYLES

The houses of the rich planters in the Antilles tended to reflect the stylistic antecedents of the countries from which the colonialists came. On the French-speaking islands, it was the French manor houses or farmhouses of the period that most influenced the architecture of the larger plantation houses.

ABOVE: *Potted palm trees and ivy grow around the front door of Mount Carmel on Guadeloupe.*

OPPOSITE ABOVE: *Mont Carmel, built in 1726, is the oldest plantation house on the island still in good condition.*

OPPOSITE BELOW: *Huge bushes with vibrantly colored flowers have been planted near the main house.*

MADE IN AMERICA

There is a striking similarity between the architectural styles of some houses in Guadeloupe and in Louisiana, especially in the use of cast-iron structures. The prefabricated parts may have been imported from the United States at the end of the 19th century.

TOP: *Crotons and hibiscus grow in front of the cast-iron gallery of Gardel, a plantation house on Guadeloupe.*

ABOVE: *The planter's chair has extending and folding arms.*

OPPOSITE ABOVE: *The cast-iron structure used for the house is thought to have been imported from Louisiana.*

OPPOSITE BELOW: *The lounge chair, desk chair, and desk in the house are American pieces of the period.*

5

THE PLANTATION HOUSE

Large plantation houses, the most imposing residences in the Antilles, are set on the islands' highest ground, from which they dominate the landscape visually and can profit from the winds. In the 18th century, the addition of galleries and verandahs that were suitable to the climate gave the great European-inspired houses an essential Creole characteristic.

ABOVE: *The lawn of the Villa Nova Great House has been planted with circular topiary bushes.*

LEFT: *The house is hidden at the end of an alley of century-old mahogany trees.*

VILLA NOVA GREAT HOUSE

Many houses on the English-speaking island of Barbados are made of bricks of white coral, a material that acts as excellent insulation because of the air pockets in the stone. In the case of the Villa Nova Great House, 900 feet above sea level on St. John, the thick coral walls contrast with a delicate, trellised wood gallery which rests directly on the surrounding green lawn.

The gallery not only provides a shady arbor but also insulates the interior of the house from the sun and keeps the rooms on the ground floor cool.

At the front entrance to the house, an exterior covered foyer replaces the porch that is usually found on the islands settled by the English. Although part of a thousand-acre sugar plantation estate when it was built by Edmund Haynes in 1834, Villa Nova Great House was sold to the government of Barbados in 1907, and now stands on six and a half acres of carefully land-scaped woods and gardens. In 1965, the late Earl of Avon, Anthony Eden, a former prime minister of England, bought the house for use as a winter residence. In 1971, it was purchased by Ernest Hunte and his wife, who are its present occupants.

ABOVE: *A typically Antillean gallery wraps around the front of the plantation house.*

RIGHT: *Stone steps lead up to a corner of the gallery that was added on to the house in the second part of the 19th century.*

ABOVE: *At the end of the lawn, an old marble bathtub has been planted with water lilies.*

RIGHT AND BELOW RIGHT: *The gallery and the main entrance to the house, which includes an exterior porch, are framed in trellises.*

ABOVE: *Curved stone benches are set among the trees.*

LEFT: *The gallery, with its plants growing on the lattice, creates an area of shade.*

BELOW LEFT: *An orchid nursery is in the back of the garden.*

ABOVE: *Two German shepherds on the covered porch enjoy the coolness of the stone floor.*

RIGHT: *The entrance hall has a floor of marble tiles.*

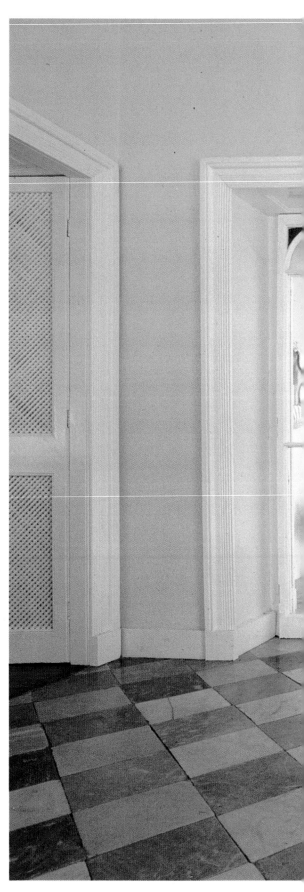

ABOVE: *A pair of dark wood armchairs and a side table stand out against a pale yellow wall in the small sitting room.*

RIGHT: *Louvered doors that allow the air to circulate through the house open on to the family sitting room. The sofa and easy chairs are covered in chintz.*

FAR LEFT: *Two unusually pro-portioned mahogany-frame chairs on casters stand on either side of a grandfather clock.*

LEFT: *An old map of Barbados hangs above a folding tray table.*

ABOVE: *A mahogany bar, a typically Barbadian piece of fur-niture, is located in the cozy sit-ting room.*

ST. NICHOLAS ABBEY

One of the oldest of the great houses in the Caribbean, St. Nicholas Abbey, on Barbados, dates from about 1650. It was designed for Col. Benjamin Beringer, an early sugar planter, in the Jacobean style popular in Europe at that time. The four chimneys are the building's most salient decorative feature.

The interior layout of the house has been modified many times over the years. The existing staircase was installed in 1746 and the porch was added in the 19th century.

In the early 1700s, when many of the colonists, particularly on the French islands, were living modestly, St. Nicholas Abbey was famous for its majestic proportions and for the opulence of its furnishings. Today it is still one of the grandest plantation houses in the Caribbean.

FAR LEFT AND LEFT: *The decorative garden ornaments are made of terra-cotta.*

BELOW FAR LEFT AND LEFT: *The terra-cotta jars were the ballast on the cargo ships that transported meat and oil from Europe to the Lesser Antilles.*

RIGHT: *The entrance façade of the 17th-century sugar plantation is typically English, with the exception of the porch, which was a later addition.*

ABOVE: *The formal dining room has been situated so as to receive the afternoon sun.*

LEFT: *A special tray table holds the silverware.*

ABOVE: *The main sitting room has been furnished with a variety of rockers and chairs.*

LEFT: *The kitchen is housed in a separate building.*

ABOVE: *The Chippendale-style staircase was built in 1746.*

RIGHT: *In the smoking room a turn-of-the-century mechanical lounge chair is covered in velvet.*

ABOVE: *The bedroom fireplace, an unusual feature in an Antillean house, was created before the colonists realized that such architectural details were not necessary in a tropical climate.*

LEFT: *One of the bedrooms is furnished with a 19th-century English bed.*

PARHAM HILL

The oldest part of Parham Hill, a plantation house on the island of Antigua, dates from 1722. As is often the case with plantation houses of English ancestry, the building is made up of a series of structures, which have been added on at different times. Parham Hill is framed by colorful and luxuriant vegetation dominated by bougainvillea.

The thick stone-wall buildings are each topped with a different wood-shingle roof. The rooms are painted in strong colors that contrast with the ornate and decorative arched doorways and columns and moldings, which have been highlighted in white.

TOP LEFT: A sketch of Parham Hill on ceramic tiles marks the roadway into the property.

LEFT: Giant yuccas line the long driveway that leads up to the main house.

BELOW LEFT: The pink house with its white fretwork is half hidden in the vegetation.

RIGHT: The second-floor gallery overlooks the garden.

TOP AND TOP RIGHT: *The geometric patterns of the railings of the second-floor gallery are delicate and transparent.*

ABOVE AND RIGHT: *The ground floor gallery is enhanced by cast-iron ornamentations in a rococo design.*

ABOVE: *An open terrace adjoins the covered gallery to create an outdoor dining room.*

FAR LEFT AND LEFT: *Cast-iron medallions and knockers decorate the painted shutters.*

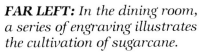

FAR LEFT: *In the dining room, a series of engraving illustrates the cultivation of sugarcane.*

LEFT: *On the landing, the dark polished floor contrasts with the white walls and woodwork.*

BELOW LEFT: *The stair banister repeats the design of the second-floor gallery.*

RIGHT: *The office was where the plantation accounts were done and where workers came to collect their wages. The room is connected to the rest of the house only by the exterior gallery. The plank wood floor has been stained red to match the walls.*

ABOVE: *Glass hurricane lamps stand on the dining table. The vermilion-colored walls add to the elegance of the room.*

ABOVE: *Three arches divide the living room in two. The ornate architectural details, painted in white, contrast with the dark green walls.*

CLARENCE HOUSE

Clarence House, an official residence for the government of Antigua, dominates English Harbour, the former British naval base in the Lesser Antilles. The house was originally built in 1786 as a birthday present for the Duke of Clarence, England's future King William IV — a fact that might explain its rather solemn and imposing look. This is emphasized by the high basement, in which are located wine cellars and storehouses, and by the rhythmic regularity and ample proportions of the roof.

The building's sense of solidity is mostly due to its square floor plan. The verandah that surrounds it on all four sides is an unusual feature in a grand house of English influence.

A system of shutters screens off the gallery from the outside. The shutters not only provide visual privacy but also shield the house from the sun and rain and temper its formality as well.

ABOVE: One of the galleries that surrounds the house is the center of family life. The wrought-iron fixtures once held oil lamps, which lit the entrance.

ABOVE: *A child plays near the rear gallery.*

FAR LEFT: *The symmetrical exterior of Clarence House gives a formal impression.*

LEFT: *The group of outbuildings that can be seen from the main house includes a kitchen, laundry, and servants' quarters.*

FAR LEFT: *The view from the house is of English Harbour.*

LEFT: *A small stone and corrugated-steel warehouse also stands in the courtyard.*

ABOVE: *In the main living room, a coffered wood ceiling lines the roof frame.*

RIGHT: *The courtyard is glimpsed through the balustrade of the gallery.*

RIGHT: *An enclosed gallery is adjacent to the living room. The white-painted woodwork allows the light to be reflected into the interior rooms without the glare of sunlight.*

93

WEATHERHILLS ESTATE

Weatherhills Estate, on the island of Antigua, is a plantation that produced cotton before turning to the refining of sugarcane. The plantation dates from 1660, but the house was not built until 1890. The covered entrance porch and shuttered casement windows point to the building's stylistic English origins.

The colors — white and forest green — are a combination often found in plantation houses of English descent. As is typical of many plantations, the servants' quarters, the kitchen, and the laundry are along a pathway behind the main house. Across the way are the sugarcane factory and mill.

ABOVE: The turn-of-the-century wood house is entered through a porch doorway. On the side, a delicate gallery is an intermediate space between the living room and the garden.

94

TOP: *The terraced garden has a view of the valley.*

ABOVE: *The stone outbuildings are grouped behind the court-yard at the rear of the house.*

ABOVE: *The housekeeper stands in a doorway near the kitchen.*

LEFT: *Overscale stone steps lead up to the front entrance.*

FAR LEFT: *In the office that is situated behind the entrance porch, an old map of Antigua hangs above the desk.*

LEFT: *The pale green bedcover and bedside table contribute to the serenity of the bedroom.*

BELOW LEFT: *The carved banister brings a note of elegance to the rather stark landing.*

RIGHT: *A system of screenlike louvered partitions stands at one end of the large dining room.*

BELOW RIGHT: *The adjoining living room also has a painted coffered-wood ceiling.*

L'ERMITAGE

The house on the island of Nevis that is known as L'Ermitage was built by the Pemberton family who originally came from Wales. Their descendants lived in the house until 1917.

Dating from 1740, L'Ermitage is probably the oldest wooden house in the Antilles. The central space used as a living room still has its original frame, which is made of a hard wood known locally as lignum vitae.

The square pavilion that was formerly the kitchen has now been converted into a bedroom.

LEFT: The wood-shingled house dates from 1740.

BELOW LEFT: The central core is the oldest part of the house.

BOTTOM LEFT: The cistern and water filter are near the building's front entrance.

RIGHT: Wide stone steps lead up to the front gallery and door.

LEFT: *Louvered doors open on to a side gallery adjoining the living room.*

RIGHT: *Dried pieces of coral are displayed on a stand that was used for holding water jars.*

RIGHT CENTER: *Mangoes sit on the verandah table.*

FAR RIGHT: *A staircase leads up to one of the bedrooms.*

BELOW RIGHT: *An oil lamp recalls the time when the house was without electricity.*

BELOW RIGHT CENTER: *A watercolor hangs in the corner of a ground-floor bedroom.*

BELOW FAR RIGHT: *A staircase that leads to a bedroom also goes out to the garden.*

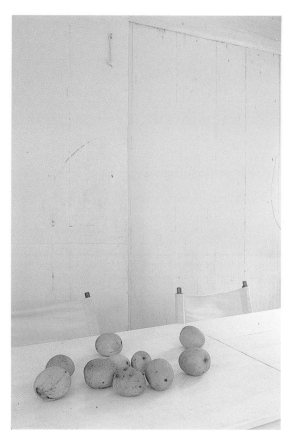

101

ABOVE: *The living and dining rooms are situated in the oldest part of the house.*

LEFT: *The framework of the house is typically English and dates from 1740.*

ABOVE: *The uprights of the four-poster bed are thin and graceful. The stool facilitates climbing into bed.*

LEFT: *A bird's-eye view of one of the staircases gives an indication of the complexity of the spaces.*

WATERWORKS

The present owner of Waterworks, on Montserrat, is a descendant of the Irish family that founded the plantation and built the main house in 1741. The simple and functional lines of the structure are typical of the architecture of the early colonial era when the new inhabitants were avoiding all unnecessary shows of elegance as they adapted to the environment.

A system of canals—the inspiration for the name of the estate—brings water to the plantation from the far-off mountains. Three types of mills powered by water, wind, and animals were once used to grind the sugarcane.

TOP FAR LEFT: *A row of coconut palms lines one of the canals on the estate.*

TOP LEFT: *The porch is centered on the main façade.*

CENTER FAR LEFT: *A pathway winds through a forest of century-old trees.*

CENTER LEFT: *A monumental ficus nourished by the nearby reservoir has extended its branches and roots.*

BOTTOM FAR LEFT: *The old canal still carries water to the abandoned watermill that used to grind the sugarcane.*

BOTTOM LEFT: *A gallery running the length of the rear façade connects the two wings.*

RIGHT: *An alley of royal palms was planted to call attention to the house from afar.*

LEFT: *A simple wood bench, painted to match the shutters, stands on the rear gallery.*

BELOW LEFT: *The walls, floor, and mahogany furniture in the living room are all of dark wood.*

RIGHT: *The green walls of the dining room add a note of color to the interior.*

FAR RIGHT: *Crystal glasses and silver serving pieces sparkle on a rolling cart.*

BELOW RIGHT: *The living room is furnished with pieces from the 1950s.*

PÉCOUL

Unlike the houses on many of the islands in the Caribbean, most of those on Martinique are not raised on stilts but planted firmly on the ground. The square plan of the 1760 sugarcane plantation house that is known as Pécoul is typical of residences on the French island.

The ground floor is taken up by a large tiled room which is surrounded by a gallery on all four sides. The double thickness of the living room walls is intended to protect the occupants of the house in the event of a cyclone. The bedrooms are located on the second floor under a wood belvedere.

The sugarcane factory is separated from the main house. The courtyard between the two buildings has been transformed into an ornamental water garden.

LEFT: The kitchen chimney at Pécoul, right, is the only element that breaks the symmetry of the plantation house.

LEFT: Rows of dwarf coconut palms set among banana trees lead up to the plantation house.

BELOW LEFT: Colorful bushes and pillars of carved stones define a walkway.

BOTTOM LEFT: The matching openings of the front and back windows allow views through the main building.

FAR LEFT: *A profusion of crotons is near the former vegetable garden at the side of the house.*

LEFT: *Near the outbuildings, a white painted fence marks the entrance to the fields.*

CENTER FAR LEFT: *Heavy wood shutters are used to close the door and windows in inclement weather.*

CENTER LEFT: *The system of canals in the courtyard was transformed at the beginning of the century into an ornamental water garden.*

BOTTOM FAR LEFT: *Water still provides power to turn the wheel of the sugarcane mill that is now only a romantic ruin in the greenery.*

BOTTOM LEFT: *The estate manager's office is situated between the main house and the sugar mill.*

RIGHT: *Red draceana bushes frame a shimmering cascade.*

LEFT: *The cast-iron bell that called workers to their tasks hangs at the entrance to the sugarcane factory.*

BELOW LEFT: *The gallery near the courtyard is bathed in the afternoon sun.*

BELOW: *The old laundry and bathhouse is now a large modern bathroom.*

RIGHT: *The front gallery functions as the living room. The ocher and turquoise hues, which are reminiscent of 18th-century French interiors, contrast with the softer variegated colors of the tile floor.*

LEFT: *Pécoul has remained in the same family since its beginnings. Ancestral portraits welcome visitors to the house.*

BELOW LEFT AND RIGHT: *The centrally placed main room of the house is used for dining. The mahogany dining table and console contrast with the unglazed tile floors, red slat-back chairs, and pale yellow walls.*

ABOVE: *The window of the belvedere frames a picturesque view of the grounds.*

RIGHT: *Part of the ground-floor gallery has been transformed into a bedroom. Mosquito netting hangs above the two double four-poster beds.*

ZEVALOS

According to local legend, the unusual plantation house on Guadeloupe known as Zevalos was constructed of prefabricated parts made in Gustave Eiffel's workshop in Paris. Bricks were used to fill in the spaces between the cast-iron elements.

The cast-iron pieces are thought to have been on their way to Louisiana when the ship carrying them broke down near Guadeloupe, and the materials had to be sold quickly.

The house's first occupant was the director of the plantation at Zevalos in the late 19th century.

ABOVE: *The tall and elegant building, made of prefabricated cast-iron parts, rises above the flatlands of Grande-Terre on the island of Guadeloupe.*

RIGHT: *A hedge of pink laurel was planted to shield the house from the road.*

LEFT: *The zinc frieze above the entrance recalls the architectural detailing in the French Quarter of New Orleans.*

BELOW LEFT: *On the ground floor there is a single large room that is used as a living room. The wall is punctuated by a series of tall French windows.*

BELOW: *The mahogany bed is a local variation of the standard four-poster.*

LA FRÉGATE

La Frégate is an imposing masonry house that was built in Martinique in the first half of the 17th century. Although the verandah was added on to the structure over 200 years later, it does not detract from the building's architecturally balanced shape and provides an added element of comfort.

The house is furnished with antique Martinican pieces made from rare woods as well as some more rustic designs from the nearby island of St. Lucia.

The courtyard behind the house is defined by a huge water cistern, conveniently located near the kitchen, an animal pen, and a building that housed the servants' quarters and the stables.

LEFT AND BOTTOM RIGHT: La Frégate, with its second floor above the gallery, is typical of plantation houses Martinican.

ABOVE RIGHT: One of the paths that leads to the house is bordered by yellow and pink flowering bushes.

RIGHT: Behind the house stands a small building that was once both the stable and the servants' quarters.

121

LEFT: *The spacious gallery, furnished with comfortable chairs, functions as a living room.*

RIGHT: *At the entrance to the covered gallery, rustic chairs and an antique table recall the feeling of a French country house.*

BELOW RIGHT: *The intimate family dining room is adjacent to the kitchen.*

BELOW FAR RIGHT: *Palm fronds in a jug stand on one of the deep windowsills. The louvered windows filter both air and light.*

123

RIGHT: The large formal dining room is at the center of the house. The strict lines of the mahogany consoles and the oval dining table are tempered by the more rusticated chairs with straw seats.

BEAUSÉJOUR

The terra-cotta tiles used for the roof of Beauséjour, a gracious plantation house on Martinique, were made from the ballast of ships that came from Europe. The structure was begun in the first quarter of the 19th century; the elaborate gingerbread ornamentation, Victorian in influence, and the louvered porch were added at the turn of the century.

The interior is furnished in typical Creole style with many pieces brought to the French island from Barbados. As in all Caribbean compounds, the kitchen is in a separate structure and downwind from the main plantation house.

Beauséjour also includes an enclosed addition used for the cultivation of a wide variety of orchids. Mangoes grow in the garden behind the house, and the once functional system of canals is now a decorative element of the lush property.

ABOVE: *A window set under the peak of the roof allows air to circulate through the attic.*

ABOVE: *Louvered windows act to separate the main living space and the verandah.*

FAR LEFT: *An enclosed verandah was added to Beauséjour at the turn of the century.*

BELOW FAR LEFT: *Once part of a system of irrigation, the small reservoir is now surrounded with flowers.*

ABOVE LEFT AND LEFT: *Because Beauséjour is situated on the north coast of Martinique, which is the most humid part of the island, the garden surrounding the house is particularly luxuriant.*

RIGHT: Dwarf coconut trees have been planted near the orchid-filled verandah.

TOP AND ABOVE: Spectacular pink blossoms and giant crotons are some of the striking features of the garden.

RIGHT: The stone tub that is sometimes used for laundry is next to the kitchen.

LEFT: A species of orchids, indigenous to Martinique, grows in a planter near mango trees.

BELOW: A group of hydrangea bushes has been planted in a terraced garden.

ABOVE: A small corner of the garden is used as a nursery for potted orchids.

LEFT: A giant tree fern flourishes among a variety of palms.

129

ABOVE: *A high-legged mahogany console, one of the rare pieces of furniture that are of pure Martinican origin, was designed as a stand-up desk.*

RIGHT: *Orchids hang along the gallery, which is furnished with chairs and rockers with mahogany frames and wicker seats.*

ABOVE: *An asparagus fern has grown to gigantic proportions.*

131

LE MAUD'HUY

Le Maud'Huy is a plantation on the east coast of Guadeloupe that takes its name from a French family who left the island a long time ago. The house was built in 1873 by August Pauvert, the director of the sugarcane factory in a nearby village.

The wood structure is thought to have been imported in prefabricated parts from Louisiana. It is painted white, as are all the other plantation houses on the island.

In the past, the bedrooms, now situated in the attic, were on the ground floor, and the attic served to insulate the interior from the heat.

ABOVE: *Bougainvillea frames the front of the house.*

ABOVE RIGHT AND RIGHT: *The gallery, with its red-and-white tiled floor, completely surrounds the house.*

TOP: *A grazing cow is framed by the branches of a flame tree.*

ABOVE: *A cast-iron bell called the workers to their shifts.*

LEFT: *The main entrance is at the end of a long wide driveway.*

LEFT: *At the bottom of the mahogany staircase stands a planter's chair. The master of the house would rest his legs on the long swing-out arms while a servant removed his boots.*

RIGHT: *The rocking chair on the porch provides a shady and inviting place to enjoy the cool evening air.*

FAR RIGHT: *A piece of wood cut out in the shape of a balustrade serves as a barrier outside a second-floor window.*

BELOW RIGHT: *The master's office is near the front entrance.*

BOTTOM RIGHT: *In the hall, two antique maps of Guadeloupe hang above a mahogany settee that is typical of the island.*

BOTTOM FAR RIGHT: *A bouquet of croton leaves has been arranged in a vase in the foyer.*

BELOW, RIGHT, AND FAR RIGHT: *In the sitting room, two rocking chairs are pulled up to a small table on which are displayed bottles filled with the customary rum punch. Wide doors open onto the gallery from the sitting room.*

RIGHT: *The house's formal dining room features a huge table of polished mahogany.*

136

LEFT AND BELOW: *The bedrooms are situated in what was once the attic. The ornate four-poster beds have carved mahogany frames.*

LEFT AND BELOW: *The bedrooms are situated in what was once the attic. The ornate four-poster beds have carved mahogany frames.*

ROSE HALL

Rose Hall Great House, on a dramatic site facing the ocean about five miles east of Montego Bay in Jamaica, was built between 1770 and 1780. The house had fallen into ruins before being renovated in the late 1960s by John W. Rollins and his wife, Linda, an American couple.

A double stairway leads to the entrance of the English Georgian-style great house. The ground floor is taken up by formal reception rooms which include a classically proportioned ballroom, with walls covered in gray silk, a spacious dining room, a small morning room, and a library with highly polished mahogany fittings. The bedrooms on the second floor include the wind-swept room that belonged to Annee Palmer, the legendary mistress of the house, whose death in 1831 marked the decline of the once bountiful plantation.

LEFT AND ABOVE RIGHT: The imposing façade and its location on a hillside contribute to the drama of Rose Hall Great House.

RIGHT: The smooth masonry wall is edged in a brick pattern.

139

ABOVE: *The dining room has been furnished with authentic English antiques.*

ABOVE: *An overscale antique Chinese vase is displayed in the entrance foyer.*

ABOVE: *Silk, painted in a motif of palm trees, covers the walls of the ballroom.*

ABOVE: *A bronze chandelier hangs above the impressive mahogany staircase.*

RIGHT: *A Jamaican mahogany four-poster canopy bed is the focus of one of the bedrooms.*

ABOVE: *A chaise with a double shell-shaped base sits under the windows that face the ocean in the master bedroom.*

LEFT: *The carved pineapple detailing and columns sculpted to resemble twisted rope are typically Jamaican.*

GOOD HOPE

Only the main house on the estate of Good Hope in Jamaica predates 1767, when John Sharp bought the property. The planter's interest in architecture prompted him to build a series of Georgian-style structures that are unique on the island.

Included on the vast property is a masonry building with a Palladian-style doorway that was the countinghouse of the estate and is thought to have been used as an office by the plantation master. The sugarcane factory structures were situated away from the main house and probably date from the end of the 18th century. Also on the estate, the slave hospital, now in ruins, dates from 1799.

The combination of handcrafted Jamaican furniture and English heirloom pieces contributes to the intimate and warm atmosphere of the main house. Although simply furnished, the elegantly proportioned rooms have a gracious, lived-in look. And now, as it has been for the past two centuries, the estate is inhabited by descendants of its original owner.

ABOVE LEFT: *A double staircase is one of the features of the Palladian façade.*

LEFT: *The main house at Good Hope is set on hilly terrain.*

ABOVE LEFT AND ABOVE: *A new picket fence surrounds the swimming pool, which was recently installed.*

RIGHT: *The classically detailed estate office is situated just inside the estate.*

BELOW RIGHT: *The once functional water canal is now filled with water lilies.*

146

LEFT: *The dining room has an exposed shingle roof. English-style mahogany furniture hand-crafted in Jamaica has been used to furnish the informal room.*

ABOVE: *Antique hurricane lamps of hand-blown glass have been arranged in front of a louvered window.*

LEFT: *Louvered panels are used as interior room partitions to divide the sitting room.*

BELOW LEFT: *Lamps and personal objects are displayed on a side table.*

BOTTOM LEFT: *A barometer hangs on the wall of the formal living room. A large dog lies on the cool floor that has been polished to a mirrorlike finish.*

RIGHT: *The kitchen, extraordinary because of its size, is housed in a separate building, which is connected to the main house by a gallery. Simple wood tables serve as work counters.*

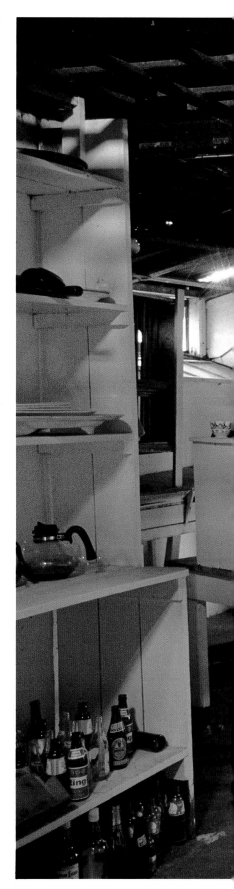

Le GAOULÉ

Situated on the south coast of Martinique, the stone plantation house known as Le Gaoulé was built about 1740. It is probably the oldest structure of its kind that remains on the island.

While the main façade recalls the architecture of many French country houses of the period, the building's basic shape and the rustic materials used are typical of Martinique.

ABOVE: *A small window set into the roof overlooks the ocean.*

ABOVE RIGHT: *The roof of Le Gaoulé is composed of tiles made in Martinique.*

RIGHT: *The paved terrace in front of the entrance was once used for drying grain.*

152

LEFT: *In the rear, the gallery, opening to the vegetable garden, gives the house its distinctly Martinican character.*

ABOVE: *A large room takes up the entire ground floor of the house. A quiet corner under the stairs has been converted into a guest room.*

6

THE TOWN HOUSE

In the Antilles, towns are hot and sheltered from the wind. And while the larger houses are set amid gardens, the typical town house sits on a narrow street and usually includes a store or warehouse on the street level, with the family residence above.

ABOVE: The restored 1912 town house in Port-au-Prince, Haiti, has for the last 20 years belonged to Lawrence Peabody, an American interior decorator.

LEFT: Houses are clustered in the town of Jacmel, on Haiti.

CITY RESIDENCE

When the house in the center of Basse-Terre, the administrative capital of Guadeloupe, was built at the end of the last century, it was one of a number of similar middle-class residences. But over the years, most of the other examples of spacious city houses with large gardens at the rear have disappeared.

In addition to the main structure, the residence includes a separate kitchen, a courtyard facing the street, and a gazebo that stands in the interior court and provides a pleasant place to sit.

TOP LEFT: The second-floor gallery overlooks the courtyard.

LEFT: In the courtyard, tiles are laid in a checkerboard pattern.

BELOW LEFT: A monumental stone fountain is the focus of the garden at the rear of the house.

RIGHT: The small gazebo has a roof of rusting tin tiles.

LEFT AND RIGHT: A colonnaded terra-cotta balustrade leads from the ground floor gallery to the porch above.

FAR LEFT: *A few hats, a bag, an umbrella, and a cane hang on a rack in the gallery on the ground floor.*

LEFT: *A collection of religious objects is displayed on a small wall-hung shelf in the bedroom.*

BELOW FAR LEFT: *The window in the bedroom opens onto the interior courtyard.*

BELOW LEFT: *A piece of mosquito netting is tied above an iron bed in the blue-walled second-floor bedroom.*

161

ARTIST'S ABODE

The 1912 house in Port-au-Prince, Haiti, is now the home and studio of Bernard Séjourné, one of the best-known painters on the island.

Set on a hilly site, the residence boasts a stepped front garden as well as a large back garden. The rooms are furnished with traditional Haitian pieces and Antillean antiques.

A swimming pool and an enclosed garden separate the main house from the artist's studio—a bright open space that contrasts with the more formal mood of the main house.

LEFT: *A large terraced garden acts as a separation between the house and the street.*

ABOVE RIGHT: *The entrance to the property is marked by a decorative wrought-iron gate.*

ABOVE FAR RIGHT: *Cast-iron planters have been placed on both sides of the brick steps near the entrance.*

RIGHT: *The columned gallery faces the garden.*

FAR RIGHT: *A trio of Haitian chairs sits by the tall shuttered doors in the rear gallery.*

RIGHT: *An old iron bed is used as a banquette by the pool.*

BELOW RIGHT: *The artist's studio is furnished with an overscale coffee table and a pair of white Haitian wicker sofas.*

165

ABOVE: *A Victorian cabinet, simple white chairs, and a brightly colored tablecloth are some of the furnishings in the family dining room.*

ABOVE: *The graceful curved staircase is original to the early 20th-century house.*

ABOVE: *Brass chandeliers hang from the high ceiling in the formal sitting room.*

ABOVE: *A series of arched doorways acts as a partition between the main reception rooms.*

ALEXANDRA HOTEL

The Alexandra Hotel, located near the central square of Jacmel, on Haiti, was once a one-family house. Striking green-and-white shutters and detailing set off the white plaster walls of the building, which overlooks the port.

Inside, the large, high-ceilinged rooms that recall the gracious spaces of turn-of-the-century Haitian residences have been furnished with rococo pieces. The wide verandahs with their rough-hewn local designs and colorful tile floors open directly on to the flower-filled terraced garden.

ABOVE: One of the sides of the Alexandra Hotel is set directly on the street.

LEFT: Green-and-white shutters frame the curved windows.

ABOVE: *A child stands on the wide stone steps at the rear of the building.*

RIGHT: *Tall coconut trees grow in the front terraced garden.*

RIGHT: *Old-fashioned wood lounge chairs stand on the second-floor balcony, which boasts a wrought-iron railing.*

BELOW RIGHT: *A small Haitian chair, painted bright green, has been positioned on the boldly patterned tiled verandah.*

BELOW FAR RIGHT: *A pair of rustic chairs, made of soft wood cut with a machete, have been pulled up to a wood table.*

ABOVE: *A painted plaster statue of a young black boy is at the foot of the stairs.*

ABOVE: *The arched window on the landing has a lunette cutout in the shape of palm fronds.*

ABOVE: *Antique dolls occupy some of the chairs in the brilliant blue living room.*

ABOVE: *The red-walled dining room, which opens onto the gallery, features rococo furniture.*

TOP: *The sandstone pitchers are used for storing drinking water.*

ABOVE: *The cook poses in the dining room of the hotel.*

RIGHT: *A checkered frieze decorates the walls of the kitchen that has been installed in the main building.*

TOP AND ABOVE: *Members of the hotel staff stand by the entrance to the original kitchen, which is housed in a separate building from the main house.*

LEFT: *Terra-cotta tiles line the stove in the older kitchen.*

HILLTOP HOUSE

Since the middle of the 19th century, the residential areas in Port-au-Prince have been established in the cooler hills of the capital of Haiti. The white-and-brown building in the neighborhood of Bois Verna is distinguished by its stylized and elegant fretwork.

In 1898, Thérésias Sam, President of Haiti, had the house built as a gift for his goddaughter. It is now owned by Nicolas Roude and his wife, Estelle. Roude, a former officer in the Russian Imperial army, has lived in Haiti since the 1917 Revolution.

LEFT: The front façade of the turn-of-the-century house is completely decorated with carved geometric woodwork.

ABOVE RIGHT: A collection of cacti grows beside the house.

ABOVE FAR RIGHT AND BELOW FAR RIGHT: The curved brick archways of the verandah have been painted in white and brown. The tiled floor dates from the late 19th century.

RIGHT: The design of the mahogany banister matches the exterior fretwork.

ABOVE: *At the rear of the house, two arched doorways separate the dining room from a terrace. On the table is a bouquet of anthurium.*

ABOVE: *The ceiling and walls of the living room were painted by a Parisian artist in 1901.*

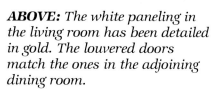

ABOVE: *The white paneling in the living room has been detailed in gold. The louvered doors match the ones in the adjoining dining room.*

ABOVE: *Two putti, painted in oil on canvas, frame the doorway of the living room.*

HOTEL OLOFFSON

Situated in Port-au-Prince on Haiti, the house was originally built in the late 1880s by a French architect as a residence for Démosthèse Sam, the son of a president of the island. From 1915 on, the building served as a hospital for the American Occupied Forces. When the Sam family reclaimed it in 1934, the house was rented to a Mr. Oloffson, a German of Swedish descent, who tranformed it into a luxury hotel.

Although the Grand Hotel Oloffson has changed hands many times in the last 50 years, it has remained popular. The hotel provided the setting for Graham Greene's novel *The Comedians*, and was used as the location for the movie of the same name.

Set on the side of a hill and surrounded by a luxuriant garden, the brick-and-stone structure gives an overwhelming impression of solidity. An extravagant series of ornate balconies, loggias, and bell towers provides a delicate contrast.

LEFT: Tiled balconies, sculpted stone urns, rhythmic balustrades, plant-filled arches, and delicate cutout woodwork are features of the hotel.

RIGHT: Elaborate gingerbread fretwork decorates the balconies of the late 19th-century building.

ABOVE: *Simple furniture provides seating on the gallery that is adjacent to the dining room.*

ABOVE: *A carved table, Haitian wicker chairs, and a sofa are outside a bedroom.*

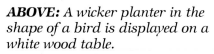

ABOVE: *A wicker planter in the shape of a bird is displayed on a white wood table.*

ABOVE: *A hoop of mosquito netting hung over a mattress provides a place to sleep in a corner of the balcony.*

LEFT: *A pillowed banquette swing is hung on the verandah.*

RIGHT: *Fretwork panels frame the doors in the living room.*

CENTER RIGHT: *A hurricane lamp sits on a table in the corner of a reception room.*

FAR RIGHT: *Plants in pots line the long covered corridors.*

BELOW RIGHT: *A collection of picture frames decorates a corner of the staircase.*

BELOW CENTER RIGHT: *Signs over each of the doorways mark the favorite rooms of many of the hotel's best-known guests.*

BELOW FAR RIGHT: *A doorway with ruffled curtains separates the bedroom from the sitting room in one of the suites.*

BASSE-TERRE RENOVATION

The painted wood building that stands on the outskirts of Basse-Terre, Guadeloupe, was in bad condition before being renovated by a doctor. All the rooms of the one-story house open on to the exterior; a wide gallery was added at the rear so as to gain easier access to the garden and swimming pool.

It took the present owner of the house a long time to furnish the interior, but over the years he managed to collect the enviable group of Antillean antiques that now fills the rooms.

LEFT: A ceramic tile-lined pool was included in the modernization of the late 19th-century property.

BELOW LEFT: The wood house can be glimpsed through the dense vegetation.

BELOW: Near the kitchen is the basin where the laundry was once washed out-of-doors.

RIGHT: One of the three red parrots that belong to the house perches on a chair.

LEFT: *The spacious gallery that is often used as an outdoor dining room is a recent addition.*

BELOW FAR LEFT: *In a bedroom, the columned headboard has been carved in a leaf motif.*

BELOW LEFT: *A tortoiseshell hangs above the settee in the open loggia.*

REFURBISHED HOME

The young couple who moved into the suburban house have furnished it with a collection of fine Antillean pieces.

The dark wood furniture is set off against the white walls of the house, which is situated in a residential neighborhood in St. Claude, on the heights of Basse-Terre in Guadeloupe.

ABOVE: *A wide covered gallery surrounds the house.*

RIGHT: *On the façade, geometric latticework adorns a verandah.*

ABOVE: *The latticework allows light and air to circulate through the bedroom corridor.*

OPPOSITE LEFT: *The rear gallery opens onto a garden planted with exotic fruit trees.*

FAR LEFT: *The four-poster bed was made locally.*

LEFT: *The shutters are trimmed in pink on the inside and green on the outside.*

LEFT: *The living room has been installed in part of the L-shaped room on the ground floor. All the furniture — the rocking chairs, the settee, and the small table — was crafted in the Caribbean. An antique gramophone is positioned in a corner by the door.*

ABOVE: *Antique plates hang on the wall and are displayed on a dresser in the adjoining room.*

193

MAISON HAYOT

Located on the Place de la Victoire, the main square in Pointe-à-Pitre, Guadeloupe, the Maison Hayot, with its imposing, wide façade, gives the impression of being larger than it is. In fact, the façade extends beyond the house itself, framing a small courtyard. An open gallery leads from the residence to the adjacent kitchen and water house.

Maison Hayot was built with the same construction materials that are used for town houses throughout the Caribbean. The ground floor, occupied by a number of warehouses, is made of a solid fire-retardant masonry. The higher floors are framed in a flexible wood that can give a little in case of an earthquake.

The interior of the house has been furnished with typically Antillean pieces, which belonged to the owner's family on Guadeloupe or were made in Barbados.

ABOVE: *The living spaces of the corner town house are situated above a ground-floor shop.*

194

ABOVE: *The second-floor landing with its Art Nouveau mirror and hat stand functions as the foyer of the house.*

FAR LEFT: *Set in the center of Pointe-à-Pitre, the building features ornate double balconies.*

LEFT: *A staircase of painted pine winds up through the house, from the street level to the top floor.*

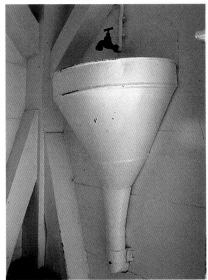

ABOVE: *The funnel-shaped sink in the stairwell was originally part of a gutter.*

LEFT: *The fine pieces of furniture in the corner living room are all from the Antilles. The windows open onto the mango trees in the square.*

LEFT: *Mismatched chairs surround a mahogany table in the dining room, which is behind the graceful curve of the stairs.*

ABOVE: *The kitchen utensils are hung to drip dry near the open grating in the water house.*

RIGHT: *Charcoal was used to fuel the stove in the kitchen, which is separate from the house. The small structure to the left of the wood-burning stove is the water house.*

COCONUT HOTEL

Once a turn-of-the-century middle-class residence on a hill above Plymouth, the capital of the island of Montserrat, the house was converted some time ago into a small inn now known as the Coconut Hotel.

Full of charm, the building is set among trees and features a delicate second-floor verandah that overlooks the grounds.

ABOVE: *Tall trees shade the entrance façade of the hotel.*

RIGHT: *The second-floor bed-rooms open on to the verandah.*

FAR RIGHT: *A bar has been installed at the end of the ground-floor gallery. The hinged louvered windows are held open by hooks in the ceiling.*

ABOVE: *The green-walled reception room occupies most of the ground floor.*

FAR LEFT: *Thin-slatted louvered shutters with panels are a window detail that is often found on the islands once colonized by the English.*

LEFT: *A single flight of stairs leads to the second floor.*

STREET SCENE

Located in the older center of Point-à-Pitre, in Guadeloupe, the turn-of-the-century private house is distinguished by a pair of stairs mounting to its door and a characteristic second-floor balcony overlooking the street.

Made entirely of wood, the house is open on all sides so that it can be cooled by even the slightest tropical breeze.

LEFT: *Instead of being connected to its neighbors, the town house with its trellised second floor balcony is set in the center of its small lot.*

RIGHT: *The children of the family stand on a balcony where pots of bougainvillea bloom.*

BELOW RIGHT: *A wood structure has recently been added to the kitchen courtyard, creating a new exterior dining room that is sheltered from the rain.*

LEFT: *The wooden staircase leads from the dining room to the second floor.*

BELOW LEFT: *One of the separate structures on the courtyard has been transformed into an open-air living room.*

RIGHT: *At the end of the court-yard, a staircase decorated with ceramic tiles leads from a terrace to what was once the vegetable garden.*

BELOW RIGHT: *The ground-floor living room has a beamed ceiling and a large armoire used to store china and table linens.*

7
THE POPULAR HOUSE

The popular Caribbean house, or *case*, is usually a rural dwelling. For many Antilleans who have traditionally owned little else, the house is the object of a special affection. That explains the care and attention lavished on these modest buildings — from the imagination shown in each uniquely decorated exterior to the pride reflected in the well-arranged furniture and mementos inside.

ABOVE: In a valley on Antigua, village houses are nestled in the lush green countryside.

LEFT: A child peeks out the window of a pastel house on Nevis.

HANDCRAFTED HOUSE

The house in Grand Fonds, on Guadeloupe, is typical of many of the small buildings in the area. The ruggedness of the terrain made it difficult for large properties to develop.

The wood structure was built entirely by a farmer as a home for himself and his family and was crafted according to his own personal taste. In keeping with the custom of the region, the tiny garden allows the farmer to be self-sufficient.

A concrete verandah encircles the building. The house, with its inventive interpretation of the sunrise motif and its exuberant use of color, is an appealing example of Caribbean folk art.

LEFT: *A tiny garden of medicinal and aromatic plants is located in front of the house.*

LEFT: *One of the owners of the house and a family friend talk on the verandah.*

RIGHT: *The bright colors and decorative sunrise motifs create a naïve tableau.*

209

BUTTERFLY MOTIF

The popular house located at Anse Bertrand in Guadeloupe consists of a main living space and two small bedrooms. It is most notable for the design of its furniture — a series of unusual pieces made by a local artisan with a penchant for butterflies.

Chairs have backs in the shape of butterflies; and the chairs, the dining area buffet, and the armoire in the master bedroom are made of a striking combination of woods.

LEFT: *The chairs and the buffet in the main room of the house have all been crafted of the same contrasting woods.*

RIGHT AND BELOW RIGHT:
The butterfly-shaped chair backs are the local artisan's signature.

FAR RIGHT: Postcards that have been received from family members living abroad are assembled on a living room wall.

BELOW FAR RIGHT: The over-scale mirrored armoire is the focal point of the small bedroom.

 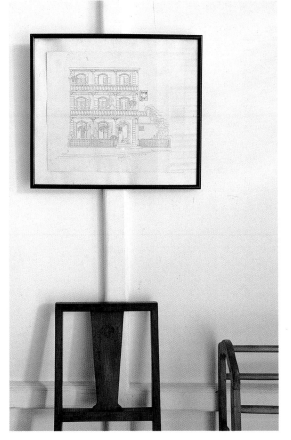 

ON THE SQUARE

The house, situated on the main square of Jacmel, in Haiti, was rebuilt in 1890 after a fire destroyed the former structure. Only the monumental staircase remained. Like many others in the town, the building features delicate iron balconies. The exterior walls are made of quarry stone and the window frames are outlined in brick archways.

Originally built by Barnabé Craft, mayor of Jacmel, the old house was converted into a small hotel in 1945. The building has remained in the same family for generations and retains its appealing, old-fashioned air.

FAR LEFT: The soft turquoise color of the frame of the Haitian rocking chair harmonizes with the early 20th-century tile floor.

CENTER LEFT AND LEFT: The metal balconies that line the main façade of the house are typical of Jacmel.

FAR LEFT: A louvered half-door closes off the archway that leads to one of the reception rooms.

CENTER LEFT: In the entrance hall hangs a contemporary pen-and-ink sketch of the façade of the hotel.

LEFT: The two peacock chairs in the living room were handcrafted in Haiti.

RIGHT: A rustic chair that was carved with a machete stands on the landing.

ABOVE: *One of the maids poses near a group of family portraits.*

LEFT: *The matriarch of the family sits in a corner by the staircase to observe all the goings-on in the house.*

ABOVE: *The walls on the second floor are covered with elaborately carved red wood panels, a popular Haitian handicraft.*

RIGHT AND BELOW RIGHT: *The wide staircase of redwood is the most monumental element in the house. Photographs of family members line the wall.*

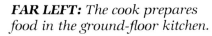

FAR LEFT: *The cook prepares food in the ground-floor kitchen.*

LEFT: *Near the kitchen, a scale for weighing the fresh produce and seafood brought in by the local farmers and fishermen hangs on the outside wall.*

BELOW FAR LEFT: *A solid wood shutter closes off the kitchen from the courtyard.*

BELOW LEFT: *A worktable used for the cleaning and preparation of food stands near the kitchen door.*

RIGHT: *Produce sellers have direct access to the kitchen by a doorway in the courtyard that leads from a small back street.*

MAISON NEMAUSAT

The house known as Maison Nemausat, in Basse-Terre, Guadeloupe, has a ground floor occupied in its entirety by a retail store. At one end of the façade, a door opens on to a small corridor that leads to the house and its spacious courtyard.

The interior is organized in the same way as many other popular houses in towns throughout the Caribbean. The living spaces and bedrooms are in the main building; the kitchen, the water house, the reservoir, and an area for drying laundry are grouped around the small courtyard at the rear. Farther behind, a small garden now replaces the traditional vegetable patch.

Maison Nemausat is furnished with a combination of turn-of-the-century antiques and bric-a-brac. One of the interior's most unusual features is the walls of the living room, which have been covered with postage stamps in a pattern that is meant to resemble the ceramic tiles on the floor.

LEFT: *Chairs are grouped in the courtyard which is situated between the main house and some of the outbuildings.*

ABOVE RIGHT: *The façade overlooking the street is decorated with an elegant wrought-iron balcony.*

RIGHT: *A wood balcony faces the rear courtyard.*

ABOVE: *An antique steel bistro coffee urn is displayed on a wooden stand at the end of the gallery.*

RIGHT: *The rear gallery features a terracotta floor inlaid with black diamond-shaped tiles.*

ABOVE: *The kitchen stove is made of bricks and terra-cotta tiles. Drinking water is stored in small, sandstone pitchers. The bread oven is at the left.*

LEFT: *A wall-hung china rack holds a collection of flea market finds in the green-walled dining room.*

LEFT: *The living room takes up the entire ground floor.*

RIGHT AND BELOW RIGHT: *The walls of the living room are covered with postage stamps arranged so as to reproduce the ceramic pattern on the floor. In the past, the house was owned by a sugar factory manager who, during the off season, employed his workers to execute the unusual decoration.*

BOTTOM RIGHT AND BOTTOM FAR RIGHT: *Objects from the turn of the century, including oil lamps, figurines, and vases—some stored in a carved buffet—are the present occupants' passion.*

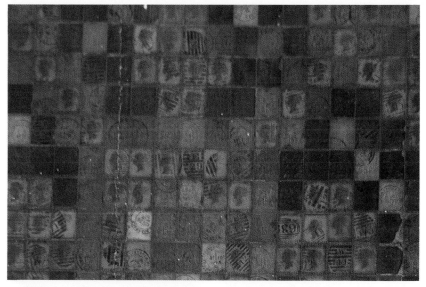

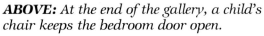

ABOVE: *At the end of the gallery, a child's chair keeps the bedroom door open.*

LEFT: *Modern Thonet bentwood pieces are combined with furniture from the Antilles in the more informal second-floor sitting room. Family portraits hang on one wall above a wood dresser.*

ABOVE RIGHT: *The red bedroom is adjacent to the living room. The chest near the door was used for the baby's layette.*

RIGHT: *The red-painted staircase goes all the way up to the attic.*

CLASSICAL GRANDEUR

The private house that is situated in an older residential quarter of Port-au-Prince is now used as a home and office for a doctor. In spite of its dilapidated condition, the building has a classical grandeur, with its portico, columns, and balustrades.

Tall louvered doors separate the high-ceilinged rooms, which have been furnished with an eclectic mix of pieces from the 1940s and 1950s. The tiled floors — a decorative design of green, ocher, and white — provide a unifying element throughout the interior.

ABOVE AND RIGHT: *Corinthian columns line the wide verandah of the house.*

ABOVE AND LEFT: *The sculpted wood Haitian table contrasts with the 1940s lounge chairs.*

CHARLOTTE INN

Situated in Lucea, on the north coast of the island of Jamaica, the Charlotte Inn is an example of a modest yet charming conversion. Once an established family town house, the late 19th-century building has in recent years been converted into a small native inn.

The exterior of the house features the delicate gingerbread fretwork of Lucea, originally a colonial town that prospered in the last century. Transforming the building from a private house to an inn only entailed repainting the exterior and furnishing the rooms with simple yet colorful and creatively chosen pieces.

LEFT: The main façade of Charlotte Inn features a delicate Victorian-style gingerbread verandah. Painted seashells decorate the path and front steps.

TOP AND ABOVE: A rocking chair sits on the first-floor balcony, facing the bay.

RIGHT: *The blue sitting room has built-in seating alcoves which are painted bright yellow.*

BELOW RIGHT: *One of the bedrooms is furnished with a mahogany bed. The old-fashioned bathtub is located in the room and merely partitioned off with a plastic lace-patterned curtain.*

ABOVE: *The wood plank walls of the dining room have been painted royal blue. A mahogany console stands against one wall. The tables are surrounded by English Chippendale-style chairs.*

FAR LEFT: *The swinging doors and arched doorway have been highlighted in white paint.*

LEFT: *On the landing near the bedrooms, the ceiling molding has been picked out in pale pink, and the floor freshly waxed.*

231

ABOVE: *The gleaming array of pots and pans reflects the owner's pride in her cooking.*

RIGHT: *The verandah's cutout wood motifs in the shape of fish heads are characteristic of Marie-Galante, an island of fishermen. The sunrise motif is for good luck.*

SCHOOL HOUSE

The small house located in the main town of Marie-Galante, an island that is part of Guadeloupe, was built by a carpenter for his sister, a schoolteacher, who is now retired. Made entirely of wood, the house in Grand Bourg was the craftsman's masterpiece and is considered a fine example of local folk art.

Although modest in size and appearance, the building features

a number of imaginative details — from the cutout fish on the porch which reflect one of the island's main sources of livelihood to the exuberant interior, where a lifetime of personal mementos create a colorful quilt-like pattern on the walls.

ABOVE: *The neatly executed grating allows air to circulate from one room to another. The teacher and students sit in different areas of the living room.*

LEFT: *The walls are covered with photographs and bits and pieces of printed memorabilia.*

LEFT: *The owner of the house is a retired schoolteacher who continues to give lessons at home to the children of her former pupils.*

ABOVE: *Photographs from students, who are now living abroad but who have kept in touch with their teacher over the years, cover the walls and are clustered on a low table.*

8

THE CONTEMPORARY HOUSE

Modern Antillean houses often combine traditional elements with recent technology. Whether year-round residences or vacation homes, the newer buildings seem to be eminently adapted to both the pleasures and the vicissitudes of the tropical climate.

ABOVE: *A hot-tub has been installed on the hilltop terrace of the St. Barthélémy house that overlooks the sea.*

LEFT: *The modern residence was conceived as a series of small red-roofed buildings.*

RED-ROOFED BUNGALOWS

When Catherine and Perro Ferie decided to move with their two children from Paris to St. Barthélémy, they asked François Pécard, a young French architect who is based on the island, to design a house for them on a cliff overlooking the sea at Pointe-Milou. Pécard, who had settled on the island a few years before, designed a modern residence based on early local fishermen's dwellings.

The house is made up of a series of small bungalowlike structures that are connected to one another by a system of open-air walkways. The thick walls are typical of St. Barts; the red roofs are an updated version of the traditional shingle roofs that are seen throughout the Caribbean.

TOP FAR LEFT: Outside one of the bedrooms is a small terrace on which has been placed a painted wicker sofa from Haiti and an antique oil jar that is now used as a planter.

TOP LEFT: A hurricane lamp hangs by the main entrance to the house.

CENTER FAR LEFT AND LEFT: A series of terraces links the different buildings. The one on the uppermost level is cantilevered over the cliff.

BELOW FAR LEFT: A huge terra-cotta jar stands by the entrance courtyard.

BELOW LEFT: Local fruits and a wine cask create a centerpiece on the dining table, which is situated near the kitchen pass-through.

RIGHT: Open shelves act as both a partition and storage unit in the kitchen. The counters, walls, and floor are covered in polished terra-cotta tiles.

ABOVE: *A low dining table surrounded by two comfortable wicker sofas and a number of small rustic chairs takes up most of the space in the pitched-roof dining room.*

RIGHT: *In the bathroom, an antique china washbasin and pitcher stand on a tiled counter under the window.*

FAR RIGHT: *An open stall shower was built in a corner of the bathroom.*

FAR LEFT: *A pirate's trunk sits at the foot of the mahogany four-poster bed in the bedroom.*

LEFT: *The small round night table is also made of mahogany.*

ABOVE: *The white gauze mosquito netting contributes to the dreamlike quality of the master bedroom. The bed is reflected in a wall-hung mirror.*

OCEAN VIEW

Situated in Reading, Jamaica, the modern stone residence was rebuilt on the ruins of an old warehouse near the ocean. The one-story house includes a main building as well as a number of separate small structures that function as guest rooms.

A tropical garden leads to the entrance of the house, and, behind, a wide terrace offers an unencumbered view of the ocean.

ABOVE: *Mosquito netting is draped from the top of the curved balcony bed. The straw rug at the side of the bed was crafted on the island.*

ABOVE RIGHT AND RIGHT: *Wharf House is situated directly on the water.*

ABOVE: *In the living room, a telescope stands ready to survey the horizon.*

LEFT: *A paved walk surrounds the stone house.*

BELOW LEFT: *An outbuilding that was formerly a stable is now a garage.*

CASA DEL SOL

It was over 20 years ago that Niuta and Roy Titus, on a cruise to Jamaica, first saw Casa del Sol, a house located in Reading, on the northern coast of the island. Originally built as a guest house, the residence consisted of a suite of rooms each of which opened on to a dramatic 100-foot-long covered terrace.

The appealingly old-fashioned furnishings, which include low easy chairs, wicker chests of drawers, and a dining room set with a pineapple motif, came with the house.

TOP LEFT AND LEFT: *The one-story house is nestled in the tropical walled garden which overlooks the ocean and is planted with tall palm trees.*

BOTTOM LEFT: *The tall louvered bedroom doors open directly onto the back garden.*

RIGHT: *A low table on the verandah holds an assortment of tropical fruits, including mangoes, pineapples, plantains, and ugli fruits.*

OPPOSITE TOP FAR LEFT AND TOP LEFT: On the terrace, chairs covered in brightly colored cotton are grouped around low tables. A series of openwork partitions lines the edge of the spacious verandah.

OPPOSITE CENTER FAR LEFT: An imitation bamboo storage unit with pull-out wicker drawers and bronze-colored hardware stands in front of the bedroom window. Frangipani blossoms are displayed in a green vase.

OPPOSITE CENTER LEFT: The wall-hung sconce in the dining room is in a pineapple motif.

OPPOSITE BOTTOM FAR LEFT: The louvered living room window is draped with green cotton fabric. Shiny ceramic tile covers the floor.

OPPOSITE BOTTOM LEFT: A carved wood panel that illustrates an underwater scene covers one wall in the dining room.

LEFT: A wood composition depicting a bowl filled with fruit has been cut out and applied to the paneled wall.

FOUR PAVILIONS

Built on the ruins and foundations of a series of older buildings, the new house on the island of Nevis was designed by Walter Chatham, a young American architect, as a vacation home for an older couple. Made up of four small separate pavilions, the 1,600-square-foot compound is small in scale and meant to look as though it could always have existed on the site.

Although the building materials used for the house — the wood frame, exposed and stuccoed concrete block, reinforced concrete, and cut stone — as well as the corrugated metal roof and the plastic guttering, were all of an industrial nature, no power tools were used in the construction and traditional methods were employed when possible.

ABOVE: The paved walkways between the pavilions are filled with earth in which grass is encouraged to grow.

ABOVE RIGHT AND RIGHT: Shuttered and louvered windows allow the living room pavilion to be open to the outside.

LEFT: A 19th-century camp bed stands in one of the second-floor bedrooms. The iron frame can be draped with mosquito netting.

POOLSIDE LUXURY

On a very dry island, where all the water is imported, a large swimming pool and luxuriant garden are estimable luxuries. The recently built vacation house on St. Barts is a contemporary interpretation of a European stone country house, surrounded by a garden planted with typically Caribbean brightly colored foliage and flowers.

A graceful series of curved steps leads up to the main entrance to the house. The open arched doorway allows a glimpse of the open-air living room and the swimming pool and ocean beyond.

ABOVE: A stone walkway and a series of rounded steps lead to the entrance of the vacation house.

LEFT: French park chairs and a folding table have been set up in a shady part of the garden.

RIGHT: A stone archway frames the spectacular swimming pool that is cantilevered over the hill.

ARCHITECT MODERN

Set on a small hill with a panoramic view of the ocean near Pointe-à-Pitre on Guadeloupe, the house was designed a few years ago by Jack Berthelot as a home for his family.

It is a building of simple proportions that synthesizes traditional Antillean architecture with modern technological developments. Although there are some cement walls, the framework is of exposed wood.

The architect decided to have a series of French doors opening directly on to the garden. The living room is a light-filled, soaring space and the open kitchen has been designed to be a convivial place for family and visitors to congregate and cook traditional Creole dishes. Each of the bedrooms has both a front and a rear verandah.

The interior is appropriately furnished with a mix of classical modern pieces, as well as a number of handcrafted designs. The stones that were used to pave the semicircular driveway in front of the house were set by Berthelot.

OPPOSITE LEFT: *A small house like the traditional* case *was recently built on the property for the domestic help.*

OPPOSITE BELOW LEFT: *Friends and family swim in the river that runs behind the house.*

RIGHT AND BELOW RIGHT: *The rectangular building is topped with an insulated corrugated-steel roof.*

RIGHT: *A Haitian artisan who lives in Guadeloupe made the bleached mahogany chairs and small side table that furnish a corner of the open verandah.*

BELOW RIGHT: *A group of modern outdoor furniture by Richard Schultz is on the other side of the verandah.*

LEFT: *Dominoes are laid out on a table surrounded by folding chairs made especially for this favorite Caribbean pastime.*

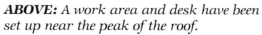

ABOVE: *A work area and desk have been set up near the peak of the roof.*

ABOVE RIGHT: *The piano is by the window on one of the balconies. Lattice clerestory panels allow air and light to filter through the house.*

RIGHT: *The dining room, furnished with classical modern chairs by Mies van der Rohe, is open to the verandah.*

LEFT: *Open walkways link the various rooms of the house.*

ABOVE: *The work island in the spacious tiled kitchen includes a stove and breakfast counter. A hood for ventilation hangs above the unit.*

ABOVE: *A stool by Charlotte Perriand and lounge chair by Le Corbusier stand on the second-floor balcony. Louvered shutters provide protection from wind and rain.*

PRIVATE QUARTERS

When Jean-Marie Rivière, an internationally known French show-business personality, built himself a vacation house on St. Barts, his primary goal was to provide his numerous guests with comfortable and private quarters. François Pécard created a compound that consists of bed-and-bath suites, as well as spacious reception rooms—all joined together by a circuit of exterior walkways.

Each of the small wood buildings was constructed in the manner of a typical Antilles popular house. But the color palette—pale pink, light yellow, and sky blue—is contemporary and contributes to the holiday mood.

ABOVE: *Each of the small buildings is topped with a red corrugated-metal roof and trimmed in a decorative border.*

ABOVE RIGHT AND RIGHT: *The houses are linked by planked walkways lined with luxuriant plants. Low balustrades edge the verandahs.*

ABOVE: *The garden can be glimpsed through a beaded curtain that diffuses the light.*

LEFT: *The bungalows all have a private verandah.*

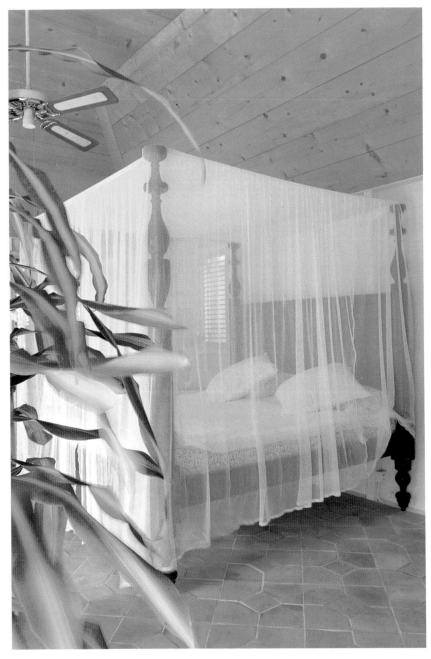

ABOVE: *A ceiling fan and four-poster bed swathed in mosquito netting are in a simply furnished guest room.*

ABOVE: *One of the bathrooms is integrated into the adjacent bedroom space and features an open shower.*

ABOVE: *The tiles that line a shower are set on the diagonal.*

ABOVE: *In one of the guest bedrooms, a corner chair stands between louvered doors.*

OFFICIAL RESIDENCE

The site, near Fort Fleur de l'Epée, on the island of Guadeloupe, offers a spectacular view of the ocean. The government guest house was renovated a few years ago by the architect Jack Berthelot. The basic plan included not only a series of gracious reception rooms for large-scale entertaining but also a number of presidential suites, which would be suitable for visiting dignitaries.

The entrance to the reinforced concrete structure is set behind a courtyard paved in locally quarried stones. The design of the official residence is distinguished by its use of contrasting materials, particularly the white, gray, and red marble floor of the verandah, the intricate wood ceilings, and the unpainted mahogany louvered doors that create a rhythmic pattern along the main gallery.

LEFT: The mahogany shutters on the verandah of the government guest house have been positioned at different angles so as to create an interesting rhythmic pattern of light and shade.

ABOVE RIGHT: The interior reception rooms open on to a wide marble-floored verandah.

RIGHT: A series of fans that have been installed in the ceiling enliven the main reception room. The motorized fans have wooden blades, each of which is covered in a different straw pattern, woven by local craftsmen.

9

THE CARIBBEAN GARDEN

For the most part, in all of the Antilles, even the small-est of houses has its own garden. And no matter what its size, no garden is limited to trees and flowers that are purely decorative. Filled with plants that provide food and drink, as well as those that are medicinal, the Caribbean garden is first and foremost functional.

ABOVE: The lavender water hyacinth is a typical island plant.

LEFT: On Barbados an enclosed garden surrounds and frames one of the island's charming small houses.

PLEASURE GARDENS

The traditional vegetable garden, which was always situated behind the plantation house, has in many instances today been turned into a pleasure garden and is now filled with colorful flowers instead of exclusively edible plants. It would be difficult to imagine any Caribbean residence — no matter how humble or grand — where plants did not play an important decorative role. Pots on terraces and verandahs are always filled with lush foliage, and doorways and patios are often framed with bushes that have striking variegated leaves.

ABOVE: A pair of ivy-covered posts mark the entrance to a former vegetable garden that has now been planted with a variety of decorative foliage.

ABOVE RIGHT: Plants in pots punctuate the verandah of Bois Debout, a plantation house on Guadeloupe.

RIGHT: The gold and rust tones of the crotons complement the dark red house at Trois Rivières on Guadeloupe.

LEFT AND ABOVE: *The garden of Montpelier estate on Nevis, an old plantation house that is now a hotel, offers a play of light and shade. Huge specimens of ficus grow over the wide steps of volcanic stone.*

BELOW LEFT: *The geometric cutout wood of the verandah, the latticework of the fence, and the luxuriant two-tone greenery of the hedge create a graphic pattern in front of the pale yellow house on Barbados.*

ROCHES GRAVEES

The soil at Trois Rivières, on Guadeloupe, is of a volcanic nature and the climate is extremely humid. These two factors contribute to the richness and variety of the flora at Roches Gravées, an ancient archeological site that has recently been made into a garden.

LEFT: The roots of the banyan trees are entwined with pieces of volcanic rocks that have fallen into the ravine.

RIGHT: Visitors to the garden enter through a lush patchwork of greenery.

RIGHT: *Enormous gray rocks punctuate the landscape of the unusual garden.*

BELOW RIGHT: *Pink flowers provide a touch of color.*

LEFT: *Over the ravine, a wooden bridge leads visitors through the rocky terrain.*

BELOW LEFT: *A profusion of ground-covering plants grows in the humid soil.*

FRAMED BY PALMS

On the small island of Nevis, a new hotel has been built on the ruins of the old plantation house of Nisbet. The property is unusual because of its situation directly on the ocean and its majestic alley of coconut palms.

LEFT: *The mountains of St. Kitts can be seen from the beach near the hotel.*

BELOW LEFT: *The spacious screened verandah at the rear of the house functions as a second living room.*

BOTTOM LEFT AND RIGHT: *The house is situated in the middle of a forest of coconut trees. A wide alley has been opened to create a view from the house to the sea.*

BOIS DEBOUT

St.-John Perse, the 20th-century writer, lived for the first years of his childhood at Bois Debout, an estate located on Basse-Terre in Guadeloupe. The property was once a sugar plantation but is now cultivated with banana, mango, and other tropical fruit trees.

A complex hydraulic system led to the former sugar mill. A water canal still runs through the garden and serves the house, the kitchen, and the water house.

TOP: *The verandah overlooks the garden at the rear of the house.*

ABOVE: *The water wheel stands at the end of the canal.*

TOP: *Ferns surround one of the reservoirs of the water system.*

ABOVE: *After having crossed what was once the vegetable garden, the canal leads to the kitchen and water house.*

OPPOSITE ABOVE LEFT: *The back garden is sparsely planted with trees and bushes.*

OPPOSITE LEFT: *Ostrich-plume ginger plants create a play of light and shade on the cascading water.*

LEFT: *The irrigation reservoirs were designed to be esthetic as well as functional.*

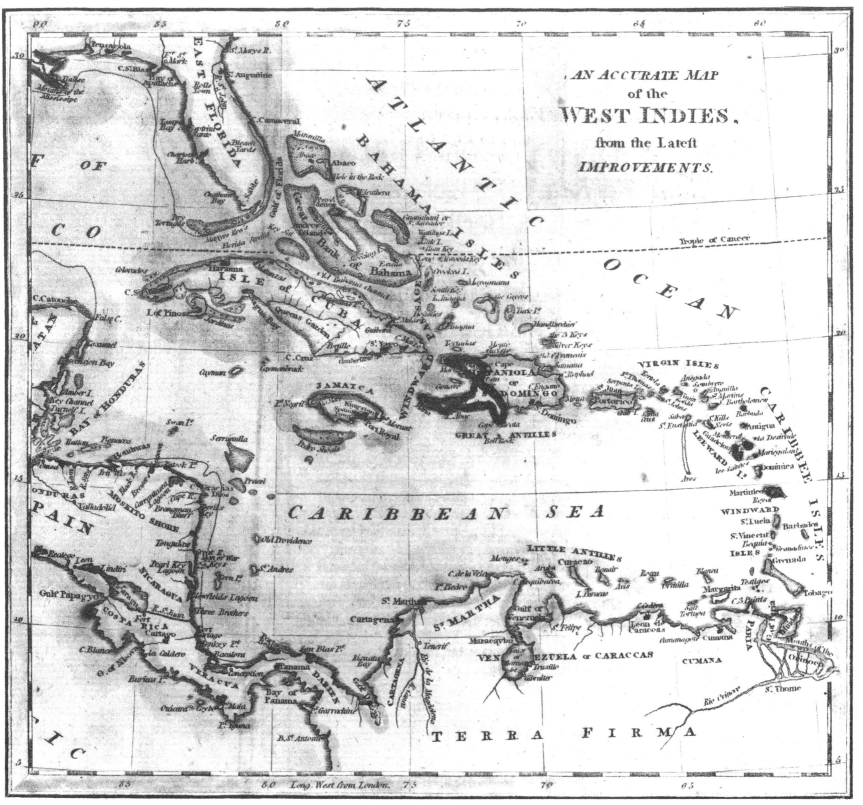

AN ACCURATE MAP
of the
WEST INDIES,
from the Latest
IMPROVEMENTS.

Rather than showing the house set in its landscape as it has so far appeared in the pages of *Caribbean Style*, this section uses architects' drawings of existing structures to provide information on the house as an isolated building type. The drawings — some of them previously published in *Kaz Antije: Jan Mour Ka Rété (The Caribbean Popular Dwelling)*, by Jack Berthelot and Martine Gaumé, Editions Perspectives Créoles, 1982 — offer insight into styles of architecture and decorative details on the different islands.

THE POPULAR HOUSE

The Caribbean popular house, or *case*, usually shelters a large family, even though the smallest of these dwellings, like the cabins of slaves on plantations, has only a single room. This is possible because so much of life in the Antilles takes place out-of-doors. The typical *case* is made up of two or three rooms, with a kitchen and bathroom in a separate structure, and today is frequently enlarged by the addition of new rooms.

The shape of the house, the composition of its façade, and the materials used for its construction varies according to the different islands. On islands where *cases* can be easily moved from one location to the next, the houses have no foundations; on islands where the buildings are not transportable, foundations consist of posts that extend from the structure and are sunk to a depth of 24 to 32 inches in the soil.

Symmetrical façades, with the main door located at the center, are typical of houses on islands of English colonization. On all the other islands, façades are generally punctuated by a series of openings for doors and windows placed at equal intervals.

Wood is the most widely used material for construction, but on many islands the simple wood frame is often overlaid with brickwork or woodwork. In the past, plant materials or, less frequently, brick were used for roofing, but now tile has become more common.

St. Barthélémy

Colonized by French and Swedish sailors and peasants, St. Barts is the only island where popular houses all have pitched roofs. The typical *case* has three rooms and is set on a foundation of matched stones. Extreme care is given to the construction of the frame and the woodwork.

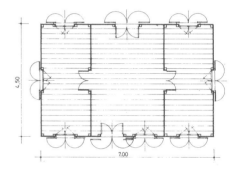

Haiti

The Haitian *case* is simpler in its construction and of more humble materials than houses on other islands. Roofs are generally made of hay and doors and windows are protected by a solid shutter that can be closed at night. The most modest popular house consists of a single room that is sometimes attached to an open front gallery. A ventilated attic allows for storage of the harvest. The house rests directly on the ground, anchored by wooden posts that extend from its frame and serve as foundations.

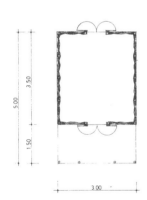

Puerto Rico

Made up of a series of ten-foot-square modules, each with central openings for doors or windows, the Puerto Rican popular house can easily be added onto. With its wood floor supported by posts, the house is like a box poised aboveground.

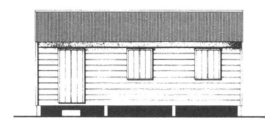

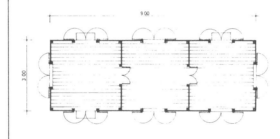

Trinidad

The typical Trinidadian *case* has three rooms, a gallery, and a porch. Grating that provides ventilation is among the decorative details reflecting the influence of the island's many Indian inhabitants.

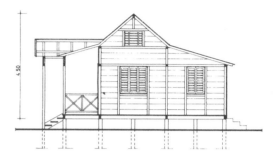

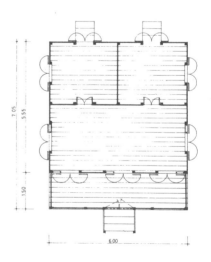

Dominica

On this very rainy island, the houses do not have galleries, and wide overhangs protect their façades. The overhangs also support decorative lacework.

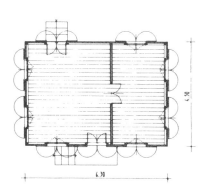

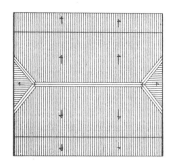

Barbados

Like other transportable *cases*, the popular houses of Barbados have no foundations, but rest on a bed of stones that protects them from the soil's humidity. Typically one room, the houses have symmetrical façades, with a central door framed by two windows. Window overhangs and an entry porch offer protection from the sun.

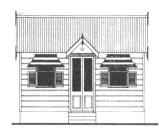

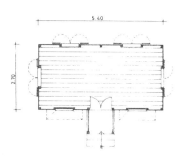

Saint Vincent

The front of the house is made up of two square spaces, each measuring ten feet by ten feet. The two back rooms are narrower and tend to be less regular in shape. Gratings in the walls allow air to circulate through the house.

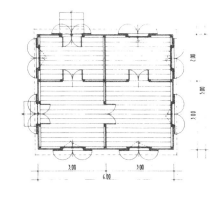

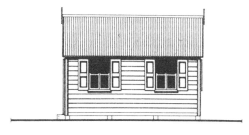

Saint Lucia

Supported by piling rather than foundations, the typical *case* of Saint Lucia is small and consists of only two rooms. The irregular façade includes an off-center front door.

Grenada

Simply constructed, even though it may encompass a number of rooms, the popular house shows a Barbadian influence in its front door flanked by two windows. The foundations consist of concrete pilings.

Antigua

The two front rooms open onto the gallery and have a four-sided sloping roof that is separate from the two-sided roof of the back two rooms. The entrance, through the end of the gallery, is often shielded by grating. The bottom drawing represents a newer and simpler Antiguan *case*.

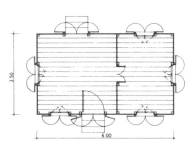

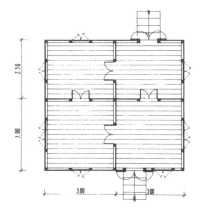

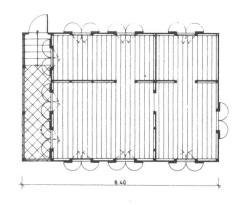

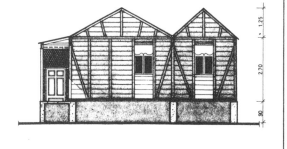

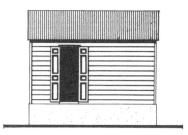

Montserrat

The three-room house with a corner gallery found on Montserrat is relatively rare on the other islands, as is the location of the kitchen in the main building. The kitchen is entered through the side door of the gallery.

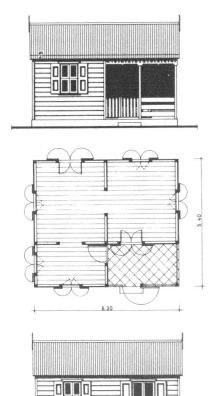

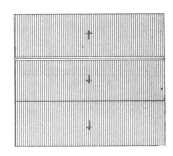

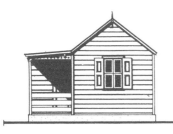

Nevis

The exterior walls of the façade, the oldest part of the house, are covered by wooden shingles. With its two distinct structures, the *case* appears to be composed of separate attached houses.

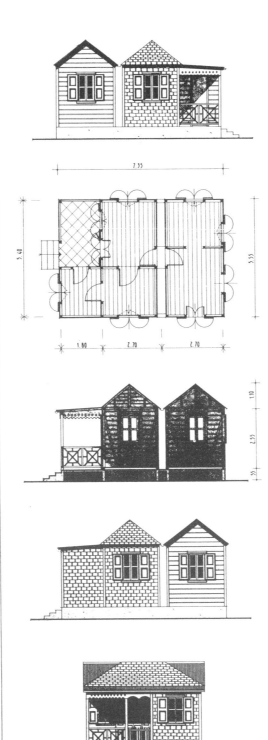

THE PLANTATION HOUSE

A product of the growth of the sugarcane industry, the plantation house is situated at the center of the estate on a raised terrain so as to take advantage of the dominant winds. The dimensions of these houses are much grander than those of Caribbean *cases*, but the interiors, usually on one level, are very simple. The kitchen and bath are in separate structures outside the main house.

On islands of French colonization, plantation houses have retained their original size over the years; on islands of English colonization, the houses have been enlarged by many successive additions. Most of the houses are made of wood and the roofs are made of tile.

Le Gaoulé, Martinique

Although rustic in style, the large house, built around 1740 during the first era of colonialization, is still elegant. Part of its stately look is due to the gentle slope of the roof that shelters the attic and top floor of the two-floor building. The verandah is only visible from the rear and faces the vegetable garden. The walls are very thick and on two sides are made up of stones held together with cement. See pages 152 to 153.

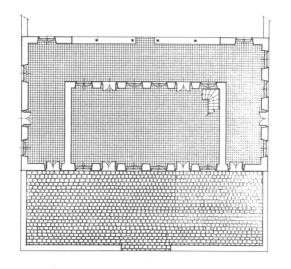

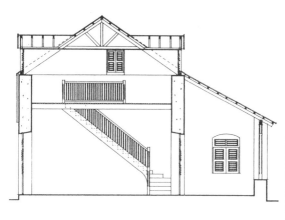

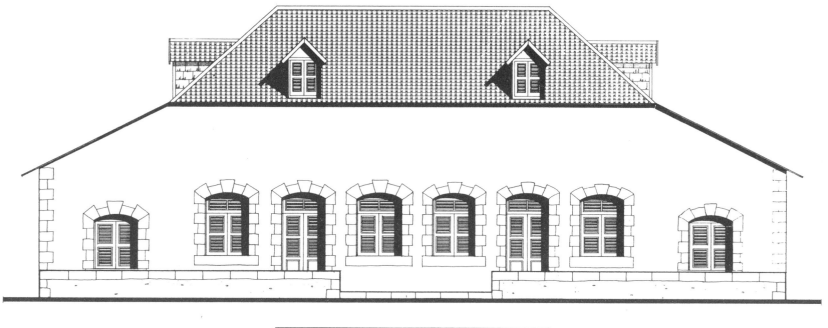

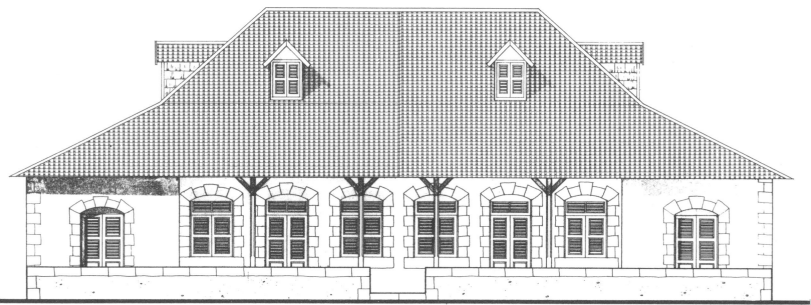

Le Maud'Huy, Guadeloupe

Built in 1873 and 1874, the house has four nearly identical façades. There are doors rather than windows on the main floor and additional living space has been added to the former attic. The gentle slope of the roof contributes to the house's appearance of stateliness. The façade is broken by the even rhythms of the doors and the columns of the gallery, which meet at the central front door.

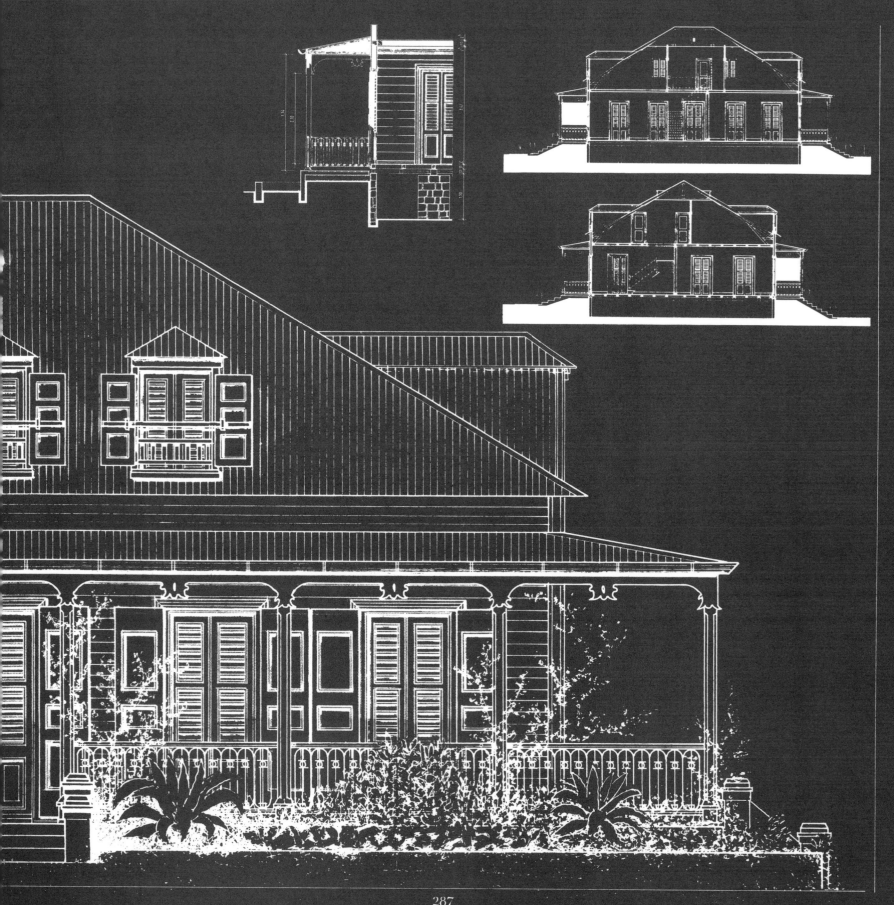

L'Ermitage, Nevis

This house, which originally encompassed only the room that is now the sitting room and a kitchen that has been converted into a bedroom, has been added onto over the centuries and now includes a number of structures. The house is today a complex of charming buildings. See pages 98 to 103.

Maison Fournier, Guadeloupe

In response to rather narrow urban sites, the town house is usually tall. These buildings typically include more window openings than other houses, as towns can be stiflingly hot. Their height and profusion of openings give town houses an airy appearance. The walls of the Maison Fournier are made of wood and the roof is tiled. See pages 200 to 203.

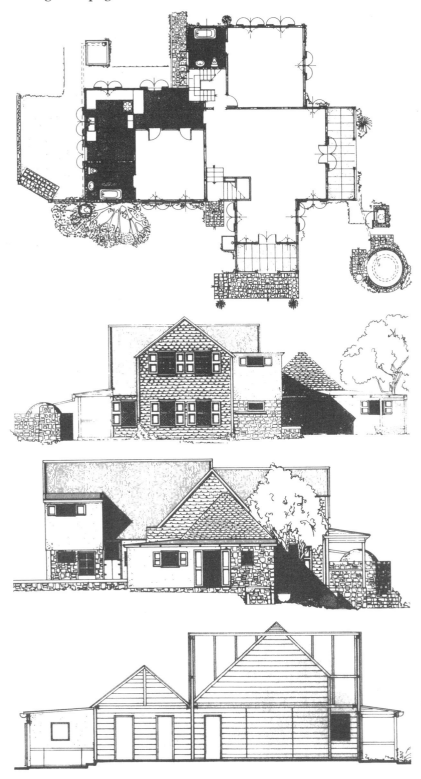

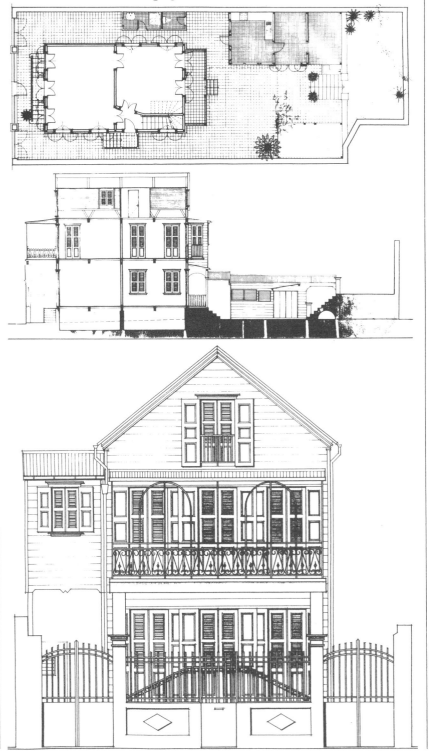